Veronica Monet's

SEX SECRETS
OF ESCORTS

Veronica Monet's

SEX SECRETS
OF ESCORTS
Tips from a Pro

ALPHA
A member of Penguin Group (USA) Inc.

For the sacred sexual that lives in each of us

ALPHA BOOKS

Published by the Penguin Group

Penguin Group (USA) Inc., 375 Hudson Street, New York, New York 10014, U.S.A.

Penguin Group (Canada), 10 Alcorn Avenue, Toronto, Ontario, Canada M4V 3B2 (a division of Pearson Penguin Canada Inc.)

Penguin Books Ltd, 80 Strand, London WC2R 0RL, England

Penguin Ireland, 25 St Stephen's Green, Dublin 2, Ireland (a division of Penguin Books Ltd)

Penguin Group (Australia), 250 Camberwell Road, Camberwell, Victoria 3124, Australia (a division of Pearson Australia Group Pty Ltd)

Penguin Books India Pvt Ltd, 11 Community Centre, Panchsheel Park, New Delhi—110 017, India

Penguin Group (NZ), cnr Airborne and Rosedale Roads, Albany, Auckland 1310, New Zealand (a division of Pearson New Zealand Ltd)

Penguin Books (South Africa) (Pty) Ltd, 24 Sturdee Avenue, Rosebank, Johannesburg 2196, South Africa

Penguin Books Ltd, Registered Offices: 80 Strand, London WC2R 0RL, England

International Standard Book Number: 1-59257-368-1
Library of Congress Catalog Card Number: 2005926955

07 06 05   8 7 6 5 4 3 2 1

Interpretation of the printing code: The rightmost number of the first series of numbers is the year of the book's printing; the rightmost number of the second series of numbers is the number of the book's printing. For example, a printing code of 05-1 shows that the first printing occurred in 2005.

Printed in the United States of America

Note: This publication contains the opinions and ideas of its author. It is intended to provide helpful and informative material on the subject matter covered. It is sold with the understanding that the author and publisher are not engaged in rendering professional services in the book. If the reader requires personal assistance or advice, a competent professional should be consulted.

The author and publisher specifically disclaim any responsibility for any liability, loss, or risk, personal or otherwise, which is incurred as a consequence, directly or indirectly, of the use and application of any of the contents of this book.

Trademarks: All terms mentioned in this book that are known to be or are suspected of being trademarks or service marks have been appropriately capitalized. Alpha Books and Penguin Group (USA) Inc. cannot attest to the accuracy of this information. Use of a term in this book should not be regarded as affecting the validity of any trademark or service mark.

Most Alpha books are available at special quantity discounts for bulk purchases for sales promotions, premiums, fund-raising, or educational use. Special books, or book excerpts, can also be created to fit specific needs.

For details, write: Special Markets, Alpha Books, 375 Hudson Street, New York, NY 10014.

Contents

Chapter 1:   The Basic Keys to Male Culture   1
Chapter 2:   The Intoxication of Being Seduced   15
Chapter 3:   Having Sex with the Lights On   21
Chapter 4:   Reverence for the Female Body   31
Chapter 5:   Learning How to Take Control   39
Chapter 6:   Express Yourself for Better Sex   47
Chapter 7:   Sexy Is as Sexy Does   53
Chapter 8:   Caring for Your Temple   63
Chapter 9:   Setting the Mood   75
Chapter 10: Using Your Mind to Arouse   81
Chapter 11: Taking Time to Date, Again   91
Chapter 12: Asserting Healthy Boundaries   99
Chapter 13: Taking the Lead in the Bedroom   105
Chapter 14: Using Ritual, Timing, and Ambience   113
Chapter 15: Enjoying Porn   123
Chapter 16: Utilizing Massage   133
Chapter 17: Mastering the Art of Foreplay   143
Chapter 18: Putting a Condom Where Your Mouth Is   151
Chapter 19: Pressure, Perineum, and Play   159
Chapter 20: Male Multiple Orgasms   167
Chapter 21: Breathing Life into Sex with Tantra   175
Chapter 22: His Prostate Pleasure   181
Chapter 23: Female Ejaculation and the Isis Squat   193
Chapter 24: Lessons in Love for Him   199
Chapter 25: Taking Control   207
Chapter 26: Role Playing   213
Chapter 27: Exhibitionism as an Aphrodisiac   219
Chapter 28: When Your Man Needs a Little Extra Help   229
Chapter 29: Sex and Spirit   241

Afterword   251
Author's Note: The Power of Choice   263
Resources   273

Introduction

The first time a boyfriend confessed to having paid for sex, I had a strange mix of emotions. On the one hand, I was shocked and disappointed that he had done something I considered immoral, but I also felt something unexpected—curiosity and jealousy. I wondered what could a woman do in bed that men would pay her for?

It would be many years later when I would find the answers to these questions by actually becoming an escort or call girl myself.

It was a delightfully decadent life choice that transformed every facet of my life in ways I never could have expected. And what I learned about sex and men was surprising and liberating.

Because I took pride in my profession, I learned how to provide a variety of services such as erotic safer sex, Tantra, power exchange, fellatio, sensual massage, role playing, exhibitionism, working with chakras and pressure points, seduction, role reversal, prostate massage, and male multiple orgasms. I also learned to assist men with sexual dysfunctions and disabilities in order to establish healthy sexual patterns.

In this book, I will familiarize you with the aforementioned topics and techniques, as well as share what I have learned about sex and men/women while performing my job as an escort.

I worked "in the life" for just a little longer than 14 years. I began my work at a mid-level position and worked my way up to the top of my field. I will share the skills and knowledge that allowed me to charge top dollar for my time. You will learn sexual techniques that are the staple of paid sexual services, as well as attitudes and information that are vital to the self-confidence that men find so sexually alluring in a woman.

This book is not intended to be the "final word" on sex or sexuality for several reasons. First, sex is a topic that you could spend years studying, only to discover that you still have much more to learn. Second, I have chosen to omit many technical aspects to reproductive biology and health for the sake of keeping this book more user-friendly (and under 10,000 pages).

And finally, writing a book is a lot like giving a speech; you need to tailor your material to your audience. Because my intended audience for this book is women—specifically women in relationships with men—this book will not address sex and sexuality as it applies to every gender and sexual orientation. If you fall outside my intended demographic, I invite you to read this book anyway, as it contains some very unique insights into men and sex as never before told by an escort. However, I hope you will forgive the heterosexist assumptions of some of the wording.

Feel free to contact me for professional advice on sex and dating, as well as professional lectures for a variety of venues:

Veronica Monet
TAP Communications
2995 Woodside Road
Suite 400
Woodside, CA 94062
415.407.2932 cell
888.903.0050 international toll-free
prospeaker@veronicamonet.com
www.veronicamonet.com

Acknowledgments

When I was eight years old, I entered my first writing contest. I didn't win, but it crystallized my dream to be a professional writer. I planned to become a journalism major in college and entertained visions of dodging bullets in war-torn countries as an on-location correspondent. But I majored in psychology instead and took "practical" positions in the computer and telecommunications industries upon graduation. Still, that childhood dream persisted when I began writing a column about love and relationships for a small alternative newspaper. A few years later, I secured a nonpaying position as staff writer for a national alternative magazine, and my name stayed in the masthead for about five years. Eventually, my contributions made their way into six different books, including a college textbook. But this book marks my transition into the world of professional authors.

So many people helped me get to this point. I want to thank Leah Learned for taking a chance on me by giving me my first newspaper column, and Ron Montana for all his moral support and expert advice as an accomplished author. Karla Rossi honed my writing skills with her tireless editing. Jill Nagle never stopped believing in my ultimate success as a writer, and her feedback as a professional in the field was invaluable. I want to thank Norma Jean Almodovar, activist, artist, and author, for the myriad ways in which she has mentored me over the years. Carol Stuart was there for me in my hour of need, for which I will be eternally indebted and grateful. Peter Alexander has shared my creative visions, hopes, and dreams for many years now. For that I am thankful. It is doubtful that I would view sex and men with such positive enthusiasm had it not been for the wisdom and wonderful stories imparted to me by Cosi Fabian. The Isis Squat sexual technique she teaches is now an integral part of my sensual pride as a woman, and it makes a major contribution to this book. Creating sexual art with David Steinberg has been a special gift and an erotic experience that has enriched and formed what I have to share with my readers. I am also grateful to Dr. Norma McCoy and Joseph Matyas from San Francisco State University. They gave me the opportunity to speak to their students twice a year for more than a decade, and in those lectures, I perfected my ability to communicate what I know about sex and relationships. Joseph Hurka offered his moral support during the dark days of wondering whether I would ever get a book deal. Annie Sprinkle and Carol Leigh, sex divas extraordinaire, expressed the ultimate in friendship when they took me aside and gave me a deadline for finishing my book. Few friends will take time from their personal pursuits unbidden by you, set you down, and demand that you follow your dreams. To these remarkable women I will be eternally grateful and humbled by their generous spirits. I also want to thank my mother for her unconditional love. I would have accomplished little in life without her unwavering support. I owe my former husband a great deal of gratitude as well. Not only did I learn a million things about relationships, communication, negotiation, and problem solving while married to him, but his love was a shelter from a world that can at times be cold and judgmental. And, finally, I wish to thank my agent Bob Diforio for investing his faith in me and Paul Dinas from Alpha Books for having the patience to guide me through my first book-writing experience.

Many more books are living inside of me. In time, I hope to share each one with you, my readers. This particular book is a humble first offering. I leave it for you to decide its worthiness. I thank you for giving me a portion of your precious time by reading it.

1

The Basic Keys to Male Culture

The courtesans of old were infamous for infiltrating male bastions of power, debate, education, and sport. In fact, they were the only women allowed to interact with men in settings other than the home hearth. While it was forbidden for wives to go to school or even learn to read, courtesans attended college and wrote books. One of the most obvious reasons these women were allowed to bend gender expectations and assume what were considered to be more masculine attributes was because it made them more sexually attractive to the men in power.

Although the men of the day preferred their wives to be dumb and docile, they did not find these attributes to be sexually attractive. In fact, nothing excites the libido as much as an intellectual equal! Consequently, men of power found their intellectual and sexual satisfaction with the very type of female they would never dream of marrying. Obviously, things have changed a great deal since the courtesans held court, but some relics of the past remain with us to this day.

When I was growing up, both my father and my mother warned me that my penchant for debate would not be welcome with most men. I was encouraged to "let men win" in most situations and cater to the much-touted "fragile male ego." I was never very good at hiding my independent and outspoken nature, so I assumed I would never be that popular with most men. Never in my wildest dreams did I think I would become a successful escort for rich and powerful men.

As a modern-day courtesan, I found my ability to comprehend the male realm and my zest for competing with men to be a potent aphrodisiac for my clients. I have always enjoyed a variety of pursuits—some that are considered more "feminine" and some that are considered more "masculine." Many men inquired about my services specifically because my website had a photo of me in the cockpit of a fighter plane or because I mentioned that I enjoyed weight lifting and scuba diving. These sports would become a shared interest, a point of conversation, a beginning point for our erotic dances.

Others were more enamored with my intellect and the controversial opinions I expressed as a writer. They enjoyed engaging me in debate, sometimes to the point of argument. This was a total surprise to me because it flew in the face of all the "nice girl" admonitions of my childhood. I never expected the independent and feisty part of me to be sexually attractive—but it was!

Although I did not entertain the idea of moderating my true personality in order to gain popularity with the male of the species, I have to admit that I thoroughly enjoyed male attention. I am sure that attention was an even more delicious victory because I had not been required to make the concessions many women feel obliged to make. In fact, I began to realize that men were not at all as I had been taught. Men did not even conform to popular jokes told about men by men. I found men to be far more complex than they are usually given credit for.

Understanding how men think and why they do what they do is not as simple as popular "wisdom" would suggest. Men are neither all the same, nor do they all want the same things. As an escort, I learned to empty my mind of assumptions and past experiences with other men and focus on the man in front of me, taking him as a unique individual. True, you can safely make a few generalizations about men—especially men from the same country, culture, or subculture. But those generalizations must be tempered with an eye to the ways in which your man may be different.

Our current society spends a lot of time defining, understanding, and defending the needs and desires of women. Women have not obtained equal rights under the law. Even the United States has not been able to pass an equal rights amendment on behalf of women. However, because of the women's rights movement, most of us at least have a cursory understanding of the issues at stake. Men, on the other hand, don't have a rights movement. White males in particular are the last legitimate target for demeaning jokes and damaging assumptions.

The most common assumption, of course, is that men—and white heterosexual men in particular—are the last people on earth who need a rights movement. Presumably they already have all the rights and privileges the rest of us want. But after 14 years of working with extremely wealthy, successful, and powerful men, I am personally acquainted with the fears, frustrations, and heartache that one can experience while looking like he has it all. Additionally, I have come to know the deep pain many men feel trapped within the rigid confines of a proscribed male gender role, regardless of their race or their finances.

As a courtesan, I treated my clients the way I wanted to be treated. I did not treat them as the enemy, nor did I assume they all wanted the same thing. I paid attention and listened carefully, taking each as a valuable person with vulnerable emotions. This did not come naturally to me. It is something my clients taught me by virtue of the fact that they showed up with their feelings, emotions, and vulnerabilities. I simply could not ignore it.

As an escort I have had a couple distinct advantages for obtaining information about men. The most obvious is probably the fact that I have known many men. By virtue of sheer numbers, I have certainly had the opportunity to see more, hear more, experience more, and learn more about men than the average woman. However, in my 14-year career as an escort, I have actually interacted with fewer men than you might think. Since I began my career as an escort in the fall of 1989, I have kept track of every man I ever worked with, and to date I have seen 1,869 clients.

I have met men from every continent and a multitude of countries, spanning a wide range of ages (18 to 80) and socio-economic backgrounds. They have come from every walk of life imaginable: computer programmers, technicians, office managers, graphic artists, architects, contractors, truck drivers, plumbers, farmers, college students, professors, teachers, doctors, lawyers, small business owners, football players, triathletes, underwear models, musicians, opera singers, painters, writers, ministers, rabbis, soldiers, military officers, policemen, firemen, Broadway and film producers, investment bankers, CEOs, self-made millionaires, trust-fund "babies," and multi-corporate billionaires.

I can no longer listen to others make stereotypical assumptions about men without involuntarily flinching and recoiling with discomfort. I often say that if I made the kind of assumptions many people make about men, I would have severely limited my income. Being open to each man's individual needs, desires, and proclivities is what made me successful at my profession.

Ultimately, I have formed some of my own generalizations, but they tend to fly in the face of popular myths about men. For instance, I have found that many men are less interested in sexual intercourse and achieving an orgasm than they are usually portrayed. I have seen many men lay down hundreds of dollars to talk, cuddle, engage in hours of foreplay, and actively seek instruction in how to please women sexually. Yet we as a society continue to perpetuate the myth that all men are just interested in doing "the deed," that they must be coaxed into foreplay, and that the majority of men are so self-centered that they ignore the physical needs of their sexual partners. I have found that few men conform to these stereotypes.

Escorts tend to see a side of their male clients that they perhaps do not share with the other people in their lives. It isn't because the client considers the escort to be a better friend that he tells her his deepest, darkest secrets, but rather the fact that she is outside his social circle and unlikely to tell his secrets to anyone who matters to him. He can unburden his heart without risking loss of approval from his wife, girlfriend, children, business partners, or friends. I have heard so many confessions, I often wondered whether my clients got confused and thought I was a member of the clergy.

The time a client spends with an escort is removed from day-to-day reality and, therefore, can incorporate new identities and new rules. If he ever wanted to try something new or different, this is the time to do it. It is as if the exchange of money frees him for that particular amount of time, whether it is an hour or multiple hours, an evening, or a weekend. He is free to explore other aspects of being human, other sides to his own personality.

No one will judge him or censor him. He need not worry about losing his job, his standing in the community, or his family. Consequently, he can explore secret desires and urges. What is perhaps surprising is that it is less likely to be something exotic that he wants the escort to do for him and more likely to be something or someone he wants the freedom to do or be.

In other words, most clients crave a break from the traditional roles that make up their day-to-day lives, and their secret desires more often involve violating the constraints of gender roles than indulging in different sexual practices. Most often that incorporates some kind of role reversal, enabling him to surrender his role as breadwinner, boss, husband, and/or decision maker. Many men welcome the opportunity to give up control for a while and let a woman take the lead.

I have spent a lot of time giving men permission to be passive, vulnerable, sexually desired, and seduced.

When someone is paying for something, you get a pretty good idea of what they really want. So the economic component of escorting cannot be underestimated. There is no need to play the games normally associated with dating. A financial transaction is fairly straightforward; it enables both parties to express their expectations and requirements. Because the male is paying, his needs and desires are at the forefront.

Initially I expected my clients to ask for sex, more sex, and then more sex after that. I was shocked by what I discovered men actually wanted from me as an escort. Unlike the men I had dated for free, my clients showed an endearing interest in female sexual pleasure, foreplay, cuddling, kissing, and pillow talk.

The client/escort arrangement also facilitated a great deal of emotional sharing and psychological healing for the men. I was surprised by the depth of their feelings and how anxious they were to talk and sometimes even cry. Needless to say, my impression of and attitude toward men only improved the longer I was an escort. I cannot take a backward glance at moments shared with my clients without feeling a warm sense of connection and gratitude.

Although men and women are very similar, male culture operates under a different set of rules than that of female culture. Most of us know this, but find it difficult to communicate according to the opposite gender's cultural norms. Because I don't view men as strange creatures from another planet, I have always tried to understand their culture just like I would if I met someone from another country. My assumption is that we are all the same inside even if we look, dress, and act differently on the outside.

Rather than take a defensive posture that says we are too different to understand each other, I enjoy the cultural enrichment of sharing and learning from each other. So if I enjoy a new way of seeing, saying, or doing something, I will build it into my own life. It's similar to traveling to a foreign country and developing a taste for that country's food or music. If you like the food or music, you will probably incorporate it into your life on some level.

A few things I enjoy about the male culture, for example, are how they tend to be more straightforward when communicating negative emotions (like anger), as well as their appreciation for being active and physical. A few not-so-flattering traits about the male culture, on the other hand, are an insistence on denying vulnerable emotions until their health is in danger or already damaged and the incessant sarcasm that tends to hide their tears.

But whether you like or don't like certain aspects of a given culture, it is important to try to understand it and respect the people who are a part of it. Inasmuch as you would no doubt treat visitors from another country with respect for their holidays and rituals and customs, you need to take that same level of respect into your interactions with men. Keep your eyes and ears open to learning new things about male culture, in general, and the individual man, in particular.

One of the most important things I have learned about male culture is the difference in communication style from the female culture. Because I wanted to communicate successfully, I needed to understand their "language." This meant putting my judgments and my preferences aside, focusing on what works. To understand the assumptions and values of a given communication style, I needed to be able to successfully transmit and receive information as well as connect emotionally.

For instance, when men get into groups, they tend to posture for status and membership, whereas women tend to share secrets and confide in each other in order to gain membership with a group of females. Experience has taught me that most American men love to tease and joke almost to the point of humiliating each other. This is *not* considered adversarial or in bad form. It is in fact a way of increasing intimacy and familiarity. This is one way male friendships are formed. When a man attempts to achieve a similar level of familiarity and friendship with a woman, he will often find that she takes offense to his demeanor.

Men also love to share activities. While a group of women might enjoy hours of conversation in person or over the phone, men are more likely to get together to *do* something. It might be golf, poker, video games, collecting science fiction memorabilia, a spectator sport like football, or a little one-on-one at the local basketball court. The list of possible interests is endless, but the fact remains that a man will feel closer to you if you share a hobby or sport with him.

One of the main things my clients paid me to do as a courtesan was to share their interests. I have been paid to do things as diverse as watching old war movies with one client or traveling up and down the coastline while another client took photos of the scenery. When I realized how desperate these men were to find a woman who would show some interest in the things they were passionate about, it made me sad. It shouldn't be too much to ask of our partners to share the things we love to do—at least occasionally. Of course, women often complain that their men don't talk to them as much as they wish they would. I believe both men and women need to meet each other half way. Interestingly enough, many men will open up and talk quite a bit—while they are doing something they enjoy!

Women invest a great deal of energy in supporting and affirming each other's worth and feelings. Our men come to us for this type of nurturing precisely because we are so expert at it and their male friends don't usually know how to be supportive in a nurturing way. And just as men are not likely to provide their male friends with this type of nurturing, they also have difficulty giving this type of support to the women in their lives. Consequently, a typical result is that women attempt to educate men to be more sensitive and caring in their communications with females. I believe this is necessary, but it ignores what women can learn from men.

Men have learned to express an unbridled sense of humor, which cultivates their capacity to "take it" as good as they "give it"—if they want to maintain their male friendships. As an escort, I learned to interact with men in this typically masculine manner, as well as bringing my nurturing female side to the equation. The result was a blending of male and female cultural components that did not suppose one to be superior to the other.

When a woman makes an effort to meet a man half way regarding gender-specific cultural differences, it can go a long way toward making the man feel accepted and validated as he is. Conversely, men can make women feel accepted and validated by meeting them half way. Certainly this will have a profoundly positive effect on your sex life since both of you are equals, sharing your differences and learning about each other's perspectives.

It is important that men and women learn from each other not only so we can understand each other better, but also so our individual lives are enriched. If you take the time to learn and appreciate your mate's perspective and to incorporate aspects of it into your personal life, like all culturally diverse experiences, it has the potential to enrich your life. If you find it difficult to take a neutral stance while you share your differences, just pretend you are both from different countries. Hopefully that will enable you to jettison your prior assumptions and listen to your partner as he shares his interests and customs.

Because I took the attitude that learning about men was interesting and exciting, they felt safe to share more. What they shared with me assisted me in becoming more balanced, informed, and accomplished. Diversity and information are always positives in any life. Of course this applies to both genders. Men need to learn to be sensitive and nurturing to the women in their lives. Obviously, if a woman feels that her man is understanding and respectful of her feelings, she will be able to trust and let go more in a sexual context as well.

I have found that many men tend to become more intimate, emotional, and trusting after they have sex. It seems that for many women, just the reverse is true. Women often want to establish communication, trust, and intimacy before they are willing to have sex. This reversal can be a source of conflict and misunderstanding between the sexes. It can be helpful to look for the middle ground in this area. The man can establish some communication, intimacy, and trust prior to sex, and the woman can engage in sex before she is completely satiated in her needs for communication and intimacy, knowing that more of these will be forthcoming after sex has occurred. Your personal experiences may be otherwise, but I would suggest that you stop chasing the intimacy and let it come to you. Almost all people resist anything they suspect is being manipulated from them.

I certainly have found men to be every bit as desirous of the vulnerability that comes from having sex; it is just that they approach it from a different sequence of events. Knowing this has helped me to see how similar men really are to women instead of focusing on our minor differences and allowing those differences to reduce our capacity to enjoy each other.

Most of my clients felt I was easy to be with and easy to talk to. They could tell their "off-color" jokes without getting a condescending or disapproving frown or smirk from me. I laughed *with* them, never *at* them. I respected them as adults. And I never made them feel embarrassed or ashamed about their sexual desire or sexual response. This is not to suggest that I catered to them. Quite the contrary; I maintained healthy boundaries and was extremely assertive in communicating and defending those boundaries. But I did so as an equal, not someone who saw herself as morally superior to anyone.

It is no secret that men are visual creatures. I would argue that most women are as well. In fact, studies have proven that women respond to visual stimuli in just as sexually enthusiastic a manner as most men do. However, when it comes to pornography, men and women often part company. He may find it to be a real turn-on, and she may find it to be insulting and assaulting to her senses. I can empathize with both views. I have made a few pornographic videos and enjoyed it immensely. I have also found some porn to be sexually arousing. At the same time, I have been offended by most porn produced by men and even some beer commercials!

It is possible to utilize pornography in your sex life so that he is wild with desire and you don't feel compromised in any way as a woman. I will discuss this in detail in Chapter 15. Here I merely want to acknowledge that most male culture includes a taste for porn in one form or another, and this is something that I learned to share with my clients to enhance the sexual experience.

Most men also thoroughly enjoy lingerie. I have met one or two men who preferred the naked female body and would promptly remove any lingerie I was wearing to get to skin as quickly as possible. However, the majority of men absolutely adore garters, stockings, thigh highs, thongs, push-up bras, teddies, and/or high heels. Few men agree on the specific type of lingerie they like, so as a courtesan, I needed to have a huge collection for varied tastes. But the fetish for lingerie is a consistent component in male culture. Some men love the way it looks, and some men are turned on by the feel of the fabric.

Don't be insulted if your lover prefers you in lingerie rather than in the nude—this is a waste of energy and emotion. A man's preference for lingerie is usually established long before he ever has sex for the first time. It certainly is not a preference specific to a particular sexual partner. What turns on any person is pretty well established by the time they enter puberty. It is nearly impossible to change such sexual cues later in life.

As an escort, I learned a lot about the male body as well as the male mind. First and foremost, we are all individuals, and this is no less the case when it comes to the male body. Each man has his own unique set of sexual responses, turn-ons, and turn-offs. Experience taught me how to assess these individual variations without requiring verbal feedback. And I learned what sexual techniques had the highest success rate for most men. Consequently I have accumulated several sex tips that will please most men most of the time. I will be sharing these with you throughout the book.

You will soon discover that most men are quite capable of expanding their capacity for sexual pleasure if they are given permission to do so and shown how to by an enlightened and fun-loving female. Exquisite sex does not happen in a vacuum of techniques. Sex is contextual and as such must be seen as part of the personalities, lifestyles, values, hopes, and dreams of the people involved. Being familiar with the keys to male culture is an important factor in building intimacy, communication, and trust and will certainly add to your sex life. Next we will look at a popular male fantasy—being seduced!

The Intoxication of Being Seduced

Do you remember the first time you were seduced? How every nerve ending was so alive you thought you might explode? The anticipation of your lover's touch, his next move, his hot breath on your skin, the smell of his sweat a sweet perfume making you light in the head. Being seduced is something many women take for granted. Many of us have never had to ask for sex, pursue sex, or initiate sex. Sex is something we pick and choose when we are in the mood. Ours is the domain of accepting and rejecting suitors and sexual advances. Most men can only imagine what a world like that must feel like.

At an early age, most men usually begin making the first move and experiencing those first crushing rejections. Can you imagine what it must be like to go through life knowing the only way you are going to get sex is if you ask for it or pursue it in some way, yet being assured that the majority of the time you will hear the word "no?" It must be disheartening at times. And I would imagine it could get tiring, too. Perhaps men can be forgiven if at times they feel jealous of us females.

The first time a client asked me to seduce him, I was at a loss. My adolescent and adult life had been spent waiting for a man to say hello, to ask me out, to reach for my hand, to make an attempt for that first kiss, to pull me to him for that first embrace. Even as a married woman, I was more likely to either say yes or no to my husband's requests for sex. After the sex was in motion, I could be quite aggressive and a very active and enthusiastic participant, but I had no idea how to *initiate* sex.

One of the reasons I never learned to initiate sex before becoming an escort was because I was afraid of being called a slut. I thought men would prefer me to act coy, play hard to get, and remain reluctant until my passions got the best of me. Of course there was and is some merit to my fears. I had even had a few men treat me with disdain if I appeared as interested in sex as they were. I think as women most of us learn to keep our sexual passions subdued and subtle because we live in a world that harshly judges women who enjoy sex enough to initiate it.

But escorting gave me permission to explore this side of sex, which had frightened me before. I wasn't worried about appearing to be a "good girl" anymore, so I had complete freedom to explore my sexual desire. And I was pleasantly surprised to discover that men also felt a need to break free of expectations around their sexual desire. Instead of being locked into the stereotype of the male as pursuer and aggressor, many men fantasize about being seduced by a woman.

When two people love and respect each other enough to be able to dispense with one-dimensional stereotypes about each other, they are free to explore their true sexual desires without fear of being judged or ridiculed. This is the level of acceptance that men experience with escorts, and it is a level of acceptance that all relationships should embody. Reversing the roles of the pursuer and the pursued can be empowering for both men and women.

You are entitled to have the personal power to choose when and why you want to have sex, what kind of sex you want to have, and to initiate sex if you so desire or to request that your partner seduce you. Those rights empower you to act out of free will in your sex life. And an important part of being empowered is learning to respect the rights and boundaries of others, too. With all rights come increased responsibilities.

I believe that many, if not most, women are less than empowered regarding their sexuality and sex lives. Thanks to centuries of taboos and the whore/Madonna complex (the juxtaposition of "bad girls" versus "good girls" that fuels competition and animosity among women and assists both men and women to label women based solely on their sexual behavior), most women have invested their sexual identity in that of being gatekeeper and receptor. Initiation of sexual activity is not a common component in the sexual language of the average woman. She is more likely to invest time and energy into attracting a potential suitor and arousing his sexual interest.

As a sex worker, I was called upon to transcend this ordinary state of sexual affairs and learn to initiate sex, seduce men, and pilot entire sexual scenarios with little input from the male participant. Many of these encounters involved complete role reversal, and some incorporated more muted forms of gender blurring. In either case, my sense of self was expanded so that I no longer saw myself as a vessel waiting to be filled or a flower waiting to be picked, and so on. Now I was an actor in my world—unashamed and unapologetically sexually aggressive. My new way of being opened up an entirely new way of seeing men. I became privy to their vulnerabilities and the very common male fantasy of being seduced by a woman.

I was delighted to discover that men want to be desired, taken, overcome with their lovers' passion, and to experience such exquisite vulnerability. Much to my surprise these big, strong, masculine men were jealous of the sensations they could only imagine as they witnessed their female partners' facial expressions, moans, and screams of pleasure. What would it feel like to be an object of desire? To wait passively while a beautiful woman approached you and made her sexual interest in you known? What would that first hungry kiss and searching hand feel like as one feigned resistance?

I found that some of the male fantasies stopped at the act of seduction, and some went so far as to incorporate a desire to be penetrated by their female lover. But the common theme was one of giving up control and being overwhelmed by the sexual desire of a woman.

Here is firsthand commentary from a generous gentleman who gave me permission to quote him:

"To me, a woman's giving herself to a man is—at its best—a supreme act of generosity, trust, and desire. I've always envied the power that a woman wields in choosing to surrender to a fervent pursuer, to—well, to put it in a kitschy way—to open the gates of paradise to her suitor and let him in. Or to stop running and let herself be overtaken by the onrushing Zeus, to wait, trembling, for the rapture to take hold of her. So one thing that I've always wanted is simply to … surrender myself for the pleasure of some admirer …. So I dream … of finding myself alone with an attentive woman who'll make me feel intensely desired and beg me to open myself for her … just to feel that I was someone's sex object, that I was satisfying my lover's appetite by letting her have her way with me. When someone's going down on me, that's the richest fantasy for me—not that I'm being served, but rather that I've been caught by a predatory admirer to whom I'm now laying myself open because I'm helpless to resist. It's about vulnerability. Vulnerability is terribly exciting to me."

I couldn't agree more. I enjoy being vulnerable and playing with the vulnerability of men. Both sides of the sexual equation are terribly erotic. This then was a major part of what I was paid top dollar for. Seduction, initiating sex, and transgressing stereotypical expectations was my job description. And it led to my own sexual empowerment—authorization and entitlement to initiate and navigate the sexual landscape—to take my male lovers to sexual highs of which they had only dreamed. As an escort, I learned all about seducing men and initiating sex. I will share my secrets with you in the next section of this book!

3

Having Sex with the Lights On

Early in my career as an escort, I assumed that men would pay for sex in order to be with a more beautiful woman, a younger woman, or just a different woman than the one with whom they are in a relationship. However, in many cases, I discovered that men chose the same type of woman over and over again. This became apparent when I got together with my girlfriends and we compared notes. Invariably, the women that shared physical characteristics also shared clients.

Another surprise was that most of our clients preferred to develop long-term relationships with us. So rather than going from one provider to another in search of something new and exciting, most of our clients picked a couple providers who were similar and stayed with them for years.

As I got to know my clients better, they would share more about their girlfriends or wives. Far from complaining about their significant others' appearances, most of my clients believed their partners to be beautiful. In fact, over my 14-year career as an escort, I was hard-pressed to find the man who would say much that was disparaging about his wife or girlfriend. A majority of my clients seemed to believe that their wives or girlfriends were the most beautiful women they knew. And if a client didn't envision his wife or girl-friend's physical attributes as the perfect embodiment of womanhood, then he often admired her in other ways.

I concluded that by the time a man marries a woman, he has decided that she is who and what he wants. Sexual frustration, a sense of sexual entitlement, or unresolved issues in the rela-tionship may cause him to have sex outside the relationship, but that is usually little indication that he actually wants to end the relationship. I spent most of my career as an escort listen-ing to all the things these men loved about their partners.

That is not to say that these men did not complain. They did. In fact, I heard the same complaint over and over again. "My wife doesn't like sex the way she did when we first met," or "My wife makes me turn the lights off when we make love," or "We don't have sex at all anymore." It became apparent that a lot of men had not lost interest in having sex with their wives, but rather felt like their wives had lost interest in having sex with them.

One of my clients was married to a high-fashion model. Being 5'4" with an athletic build, I don't resemble a high-fashion model. I remember being intrigued that a man married to a model would retain the services of an escort at all, let alone one that was petite and muscular. Perhaps in his case he *did* want something different. Or perhaps he, like a lot of men, felt that his wife had lost interest in sex with him. I only know that he complained about her. His big complaint? She worried about walking up a slight hill because it might build muscles in her calves and ruin her emaciated look.

I had occasion to see a photo of a client's wife. I visited him in their home while she was away on business. She was an incredibly beautiful woman. And, again, I wondered why would a man want to pay for sex when his wife is such a beautiful woman? Of course, since the arrest of actor Hugh Grant for soliciting a prostitute while he was dating the gorgeous actress Elizabeth Hurley, it isn't all that shocking. But it still points to the error in some popular assumptions about what men want and why they pay for sex.

One erroneous assumption is that all men find the same type of female sexually attractive. Men perpetuate this misnomer when they are in the company of their male friends. Admitting that you don't find a woman attractive, when she conforms to the current cultural dictates of beauty, can set a man up to be teased for being "gay" or otherwise less than masculine. And if a man were to tell his male friends that he was attracted to a woman who deviates from the accepted standards of beauty, he would risk humiliation at the hands of his so-called friends.

The taboo against being sexually attracted to anyone considered inappropriate is powerful for both men and women. Men tend to talk about which women they would have sex with when they are in groups, and one of the ways that they compete is by professing superior standards. Men also tend to bond over this perceived sharing of their mutual attraction for particular females or certain types of females.

For instance, a woman might walk by while they are talking, and then someone in the group would say something about how much he would love to "do her." The male bonding and affirmation of their heterosexuality occurs when all the other men agree that they would love to have sex with her, too. To take this past male bonding and turn it into a competition, some men will brag that they wouldn't consider having sex with her because of any number of imagined physical flaws. This is partly a case of "sour grapes" (I don't stand a chance at having sex with this woman so I will simply convince myself that I don't want to have sex with her) and partly a way to embarrass the guy who said he would have sex with her. If a member of the group does not seem as picky as the others, he is deemed desperate.

Remember men bond by mercilessly teasing each other (see Chapter 1). Unfortunately, they also tend to buy into their own nonsense. It never occurs to the men engaged in this game of one-upmanship that their friend may genuinely find a different type of female body beautiful, regardless of how accessible she may or may not be. After you take the scenario out of the realm of imagination and find out what men actually spend their money on, the vast variety of male preferences in women reveals itself. Out of a world of limitless choices, men who see escorts tend to have very definite preferences, and these are not always in line with media representations of beauty.

When his friends aren't looking, many men will choose to have sex with a woman who does not conform to the standards for which he and his buddies profess admiration—even when they could easily pay for sex with a woman that did conform to those standards. I think this is a testament to how complex men are, and it is nice to know there is something to that old adage that "there is someone for everyone."

Women also make some assumptions about what men want in a woman, and a very popular assumption is that all men want women to be skinny. Women's magazines are full of photos of starving pubescent girls passing as the ideal for adult women's bodies. Over the past several decades, the female "ideal" has morphed into what more closely resembles a postoperative male to female transsexual than a genetic adult female. Impossibly narrow hips supported by stick legs and topped off with huge breasts is not how the natural female body is constructed, except in the rarest of cases. Women in their reproductive years are intended by nature to have some fat on their hips and thighs to support the development of a baby. Too little body fat can shut down a woman's menstrual cycle entirely.

Fortunately, in the interest of continuing the human species, men have been programmed by nature to respond favorably to a healthy natural female body. Although most women feel that men's magazines promote idealized and unrealistic images of the female body, a noticeable difference exists between women's and men's magazines.

The women's magazines have far more anorexic images than the men's magazines. So although both men and women buy magazines with photos of their ideal female form, the popular men's magazines prefer women who look like they have enough meat on them that they could actually get pregnant. Most fashion photos in women's magazines show females who look like they are about to collapse from hunger or too much heroin.

There are also men's magazines that cater to specific tastes. Some men love very hairy women. Some men love tiny breasts.

Some men love huge breasts. Some men love blondes. Some men love redheads. Some men love brunettes. Some men love fat. There are men's magazines for all of these female attributes and then some.

If a given man has an attraction to a particular type of female body, he is not likely to deviate from that. What any of us finds sexy is often implanted in our brain at a very early age. It is not an easy task to reprogram what turns us on. Some would say it is next to impossible.

The affair between President Bill Clinton and Monica Lewinsky illustrates several of the aforementioned points. First off, as the most powerful man on the planet, Bill Clinton could have had sex with any woman he wanted to—and he did. What so many fail to realize is that he was not in any way settling when he chose his sexual partners. This was not a case of low self-esteem or someone who lacked what it takes to get what he wants in life. Bill Clinton is used to having high aspirations and watching them turn into successful accomplishments. If he had wanted what some men think he should have wanted in the way of a female sexual partner—he would have gotten it.

But Bill Clinton is not attracted to what others may think he should find attractive. He obviously loves women who have generous hips, large sexy eyes, and big beautiful smiles. As an escort, I know that after a man has decided that he prefers a particular body type in women, he will tend to stick with that for the rest of his life. It doesn't matter what is popular or in fashion this year.

The beauty a man sees in a woman is timeless unless, of course, he really is suffering from low self-esteem. Then, unfortunately, he will care too much about what other people think to stay true to himself and his desires. I had clients like that, too. They came to see me just because my body fit a certain stereotypical ideal or because they had seen me on television or in an adult video. They were concerned with attaining a fantasy of what they thought they should want—something that might impress their friends or make them feel more secure about themselves. Men who choose their sexual partners based upon what others think don't enjoy the sex all that much, so I don't recommend it.

The world of escorts is full of surprises. One thing that shocked me was just how diverse successful escorts are. Some stereotypes do hold true to some extent. White women tend to attract more clients and higher prices than women of color. No one can say that the market that drives the sex industry is any less racist than the rest of the world. And obese women are not in as high demand as fit females. Similarly, younger women make more money than older women—usually—not always.

But that said, a huge variety of women are making money as escorts. The business of escorting is driven by the libido of men, and given the diverse physical characteristics of escorts one can safely assume that men enjoy sex with a lot of different types of women. As previously stated, most men prefer one physical type of woman, and they can be extremely specific. But each man is different and so are his preferences. The clients of skinny women are not usually the clients of obese women. But both body types *do* have clients. Women who are older have clients. Women who are very hairy have clients. Women of just about any physical description do work as escorts.

Some may have more clients than others, and it may be tempting to say this has something to do with the way they look. But I have found that this is not always true. I know of several women who would be considered old or fat by society's current standards who are making more money than many skinny, busty blondes. This fact should come as good news to women who are not escorts, because it suggests that many men appreciate you exactly as you are.

But it isn't just about women's bodies. Men pay to have sex with women for reasons that transcend their appearance. Just what are those reasons? The answer to that question is complex, as this book suggests. One thing men love about escorts is how much escorts love themselves. Escorts dress up in lingerie and burst into the room like a diva! They may strut their stuff or play coy, but the bottom line is that the lights stay on! An escort is proud of her body, no matter what it looks like. She is familiar with her strong points, and her confidence translates to an irresistible sex appeal.

If you don't already, I hope that you will begin to feel that same level of body confidence. One of the reasons escorts feel so sexy is the fact that so many men tell us we are, both in words and in dollars. Thanks to years of negative messages from the media and the culture, *all* women feel self-conscious and inadequate about their bodies. Even supermodels admit to these feelings (and I wouldn't mention this but for the fact that our culture holds them up as an ideal). Hopefully, as you read the truth about men's sexual desires and preferences, you will come to realize that these negative messages have more to do with marketing than they do with biology. The good news is that your man no doubt already thinks you are sexy. He is probably just waiting for you to agree with him.

4

Reverence for the Female Body

When the Playboy channel came to film a documentary about my life and work, I was asked to act out a couple of typical appointments with clients. In one scene I asked the male model to pantomime worshipping my body—something for which many of my clients paid good money. It wasn't that I was a unique escort who was being afforded this special treatment by her clients; quite the contrary. In my business, everyone knows what the term "body worship" means, and it usually evokes contented smiles among the women.

Before becoming an escort, I would have never in my wildest dreams guessed that men wanted to show reverence for women's bodies with this level of enthusiasm. It was something one had to see to believe. Even men who did not refer to this activity as "body worship" would bring elements of it to our time together. A degree of awe and respect often overtakes men when they are in the presence of the naked female form. And, yet, we women either take it for granted or seem not to notice.

At first I wondered why I had so rarely encountered this male sexual obsession before becoming an escort. Looking back on my nonprofessional encounters, I began to see that, in fact, some body worship had existed but I had not noticed it. I was usually way too uncomfortable about being naked to enjoy having my body worshipped. I couldn't fathom just lying there and being attended to with so much passion. So I usually interrupted the man and tried to make sure I was performing some sex act on him or with him in the interest of maintaining the "give and take."

I was uncomfortable being the center of attention like that. I preferred that my male partner was enjoying himself. I wasn't self-sacrificing—just self-conscious. And besides, it did seem kind of selfish to just lay there and be admired. It never occurred to me that the presence of my naked female body was gift enough. Thankfully, many men were willing to teach me just how special women's bodies are and how grateful they can be to explore, enjoy, and experience us from head to toe!

To my surprise, much of this adoration centers on the female genitals. After all those years of thinking that female genitals were less than attractive or sexy—that they might even be considered disgusting or dirty by some—I was now finding out that many men consider female genitals on a par with legendary works of art like the Sistine Chapel. Experience has taught me that women's genitals evoke the same spiritual high in most men that great art does for many people. The look on men's faces when they see women's genitals is unmistakable. It can only be described as awe. They may have seen many different women naked, but it seems their fascination and profound regard never wavers.

Escorts who envision a spiritual dimension to their work actually believe they are getting paid as sacred prostitutes to allow worshipful access to their vulva. They demand and expect the level of respect and reverence you would ordinarily associate with a church service. And many men are only too happy to oblige. In fact, it seems this is an important activity for many men—something they feel a need for—something that is not allowed for in other aspects of their daily lives and relationships.

Unfortunately, some women are so self-conscious about their bodies that they may never know how much their men may long to explore and/or worship their naked frames. I have met more than a few men who, although married for years, were not terribly familiar with the female body. It wasn't for lack of interest or lack of trying. Apparently their wives did not encourage their curiosity, so they had to pay a professional to learn simple anatomy such as the location of the clitoris. Now if these same men simply did not care about providing women with sexual pleasure, it is doubtful they would have paid hard-earned cash to purchase lessons in pleasing women. Fortunately, I have found men to be much more considerate and anxious to satisfy women than they are usually given credit for.

Of course, a few men really don't have a clue that women are complex sexual creatures capable of enormous sexual pleasure. And these are often the same men who have no idea that they are also capable of increased sexual pleasure. Because they approach sex as though it were as uncomplicated a procedure as eating your dinner in front of the television set, they may need a little prompting to get out of their ill-informed sexual rut. You might begin by highlighting your favorite lines from this book and then reading a couple short sentences to him to see whether you can spark his interest.

The point is to introduce the idea of sex as something that is learned and something he may not know all there is to know about. After he has digested that bit of news, you can move on to telling him how you like it. Be sure to read Chapter 24 for some tips on how to do that!

A lot of my work as an escort was spent teaching men who were hungry for information on the fine art of pleasuring a woman. They wanted to know everything—where the clitoris is, how to find the G-spot, what female ejaculation is, how to perform cunnilingus, how they should touch breasts (it really depends upon the woman, of course), and so on. So these supposedly selfish brutes who only care about getting off were literally taking classes in how to please women. Because most men are so performance oriented, I find it hard to believe there are many men who don't care about their performance in bed. It is a source of a great deal of anxiety for most men. Certainly most of the men I have met over the years were completely aware of the fact that sex is better if you learn more, and they couldn't wait to become better at it!

The good news for us women is that all we have to do is get past our own embarrassment or feelings of being less than worthy and give men a chance to show us a good time! Most men really do want to please us if only they knew how. And if your man does not ask you to tell him how to please you, you can simply tell him what you want. It is best to do this before you are actually engaged in sexual activity. A little advanced warning goes a long way to assuage any possible hurt feelings on his part. Don't broach the topic by telling him how you have been faking orgasms or how some other lover did it better. Be polite and respectful and approach the topic trusting that he really does care how you feel and what you want. As long as he does not feel like you are talking down to him, you are sure to be rewarded with at least an enthusiastic attempt.

Some men do have trouble following directions. It may take a few attempts to get your message across, but don't give up. Some creative ways you can communicate your needs include showing him pictures and/or diagrams in a book about sexual positions and techniques, watching a pornographic movie that contains the activity you desire, drawing him a picture, or using metaphors. However, the most effective way to talk about sex is usually in as straightforward and honest a fashion as possible.

For instance, when I am trying to teach a man to perform perfect cunnilingus I instruct him to avoid drooling, as the excess saliva feels perfectly awful to me. I tell him to move his tongue around or hold his tongue still and move his head, but never lap my genitals like animals lap water, because I don't like the way that feels. And be sure to stop touching my clitoris right after I have an orgasm because it is too sensitive to be touched at that time.

Although I am very clear, concise, and to the point, I maintain a soft or humorous approach. I keep in mind that he wants the information, but he doesn't want to feel foolish. It is a fine line between delivering the message and delivering a blow to his pride. Humor can be very helpful. If you can share a laugh while you discuss your sexual desires, it takes the discussion into a mutual arena instead of an adversarial one. It really is as simple as speaking to him in the same way in which you would want to be spoken.

One mistake in sexual technique that is rather common among men is that of being far too rough with a woman's body—especially her genitals. Now this is not because men are selfish or inconsiderate. Quite the contrary; they are adhering to the Golden Rule—treat others as you would want to be treated. Many men love to have their penis handled firm and fast—the rougher the better. They even have terms like "spanking" it and "jerking off" that accentuate this rough treatment of the penis. So a man who has not been told otherwise is likely to touch the woman's clitoris the same way he would want you to touch his penis—fast and firm.

Most women do not find it pleasurable to have their clitoris touched in a rough way. Because we have as many nerve endings in the tiny tip of our clitoris as men have in the comparatively large glans (head) of their penis, the clitoris is a very sensitive sex organ that does not require as much tactile stimulation to produce as much pleasure. This difference in anatomy and sexual response becomes a perfect opportunity to share information and to practice telling him what you want sexually.

And because even women differ in sexual preferences and sexual response, a man who has learned to please one woman will not necessarily know how to please the next woman. This variation in sexual response is also true of men, so be sure to invite your man to tell you what he likes and doesn't like, too. It is vitally important that couples learn to talk about sex with each other and communicate their desires to one another. This is the only way we can know whether we are, in fact, connected in a sexually authentic and mutually pleasurable way. (Be sure to read Chapter 24 for extremely detailed instructions on how to tell your man what turns you on!)

In summary, I learned that men want to be seduced by women; that they enjoy having sex with women who love their own bodies and aren't embarrassed to show off; and that men are infinitely curious about female anatomy and want to worship our genitals. But the last thing I learned about men was perhaps the most shocking: men want to stop being men for a few hours—especially during sex. Not that they want to stop having male anatomy, but they want to stop playing their proscribed gender role. They crave a little role reversal! And that's the topic of the next chapter.

5

Learning How to Take Control

When I first started working as an escort, I assumed that I would be doing what my clients told me to do. After all, I had to follow the instructions of my employer as long as they were signing my paychecks! But I was wrong. My clients assumed I was the professional, and they were paying me to know what I was doing and to take control of our time together. At first I was rather lost. But I quickly learned to enjoy this new role in relation to men.

I am convinced that this dynamic does not have to be limited to a professional relationship. In fact, the constant pressure to make decisions at work and at home seems to be a source of anxiety and fatigue for many men. They want a break from it. But how do you ask your wife or girlfriend to take a more masculine role in the relationship once in a while without risking the loss of her respect and trust?

Many women expect their man to provide them with the sense of security and safety that is provided by the stereotypical male role. We want our men to be strong, brave, and impervious to pain, just like our heroes in the movies. And, as women, we can get pretty spoiled expecting our men to seduce us, make love to us, provide us with earth-shaking orgasms, and rub our feet or back afterward, preferably while cuddling and sharing their deepest emotions.

Sometimes men also want to be seduced, to be made love to, to have earth-shaking orgasms followed by massage and gentle conversation. Yet this treatment qualifies as role reversal simply because stereotypical female behavior is one of waiting, being receptive, and perhaps demanding that he cater to us because we have been so generous as to grant him sexual access.

In an effort to preserve our pride and "good girl" status, many of us have adopted a rather aloof stance sexually. We make him work for it. We don't express our lust or our enthusiasm, and we certainly don't make the first move, or the second, or the third …. On the other hand, some women—especially younger women—are much too eager to please and cater to men sexually. They may not have learned to pursue their own sexual pleasure and so may be more likely to engage in sex acts just to stimulate the male. This can be anything from oral sex to girl/girl sex, and if it is not something that actually turns the woman on, she is setting herself up for major disappointment.

None of us has much respect for anyone who is less than authentic. It comes off as manipulative at best and usually communicates a lack of self-respect. Manipulation also negates every woman's right to be pleased sexually. But most importantly, it transforms sexual interaction from an opportunity for intimacy and physical pleasure to a bid for attention and approval.

The desire to fit in, be liked, or feel popular is *not* a good reason to engage in any sexual behavior. Unfortunately, it can be a motivation for having sex for some women. Although the promiscuous behavior of some younger women seems completely opposed to the almost frigid role their grandmothers may have played in the past, there are actually quite a few similarities.

Years ago, women were instructed to have sex with their husbands whether they wanted to or not in order to fulfill their "wifely duty." In fact, it was assumed that women would not want to have sex of their own free will. Sex was thought of as a disgusting act a woman endured simply to satisfy the man's carnal desires.

Modern sexuality following the sexual revolution of the 1960s may appear to be open and egalitarian, but in fact it is just another incarnation of the same oppressive attitude about sexuality. The general consensus is still that men desire sex more than women do. And we have few cultural norms that communicate the authentic sexual desires of women. So when women attempt to break free of old sexual taboos, they may be hard-pressed to know how to do it without catering to male desire. Young women who want to embrace their own sexual desire don't have any healthy role models to emulate, so they end up expressing a sexual fantasy that is male-centric.

A male-centric view of sex is more likely to focus on giving a great blow job without showing any interest or desire for cunnilingus. A male-centric view of sex is more likely to emphasize the woman's body as either beautiful or in need of improvements while ignoring the male body as being capable of providing visual attraction or repulsion. A male-centric approach to sex emphasizes the female's role in stimulating and pleasing the male while remaining oblivious to the mechanisms for female sexual satisfaction.

It is important to strike a healthy balance and avoid extremes. Whether a woman is playing "hard to get" and demanding that her man give her 10 orgasms after she "allows" him to have sex with her or a woman is striving to impress a man with her bold and enthusiastic fellatio techniques and pantomimed interest in "girl/girl" sex without any regard for what truly turns her on, she is ultimately losing herself in the bargain. It may be appropriate to negotiate fantasy role play to turn on your partner, but this should not become a substitute for the expression of your authentic sexual desire. If you end up acting your way through your entire sex life, you will never be true to yourself.

To begin to own your sexual desires and pleasure—independent of what the proverbial "they" or "he" may think—you have to start talking about and exploring what truly turns you on. Get familiar with your own body and sexual responses. And ultimately, you must take responsibility for achieving orgasms instead of blaming him or forgetting that you have sexual needs, too. Start initiating sex, at least part of the time, instead of always waiting for him to "pick you" or "making him work for it." A woman can learn a lot about her own sexual desire by initiating sex, and happily this is also a turn-on for men. So it can be a win/win situation!

One of the things my clients loved about time with me was that I never asked them what they wanted. I just told them to lay back and enjoy the ride. I got very good at sizing up men sexually so I could determine the best way to treat a man without him having to say a word. Certainly, if you are in a long-term relationship it should not require any special skills to familiarize yourself with your partner's likes and dislikes. If you know him at all, you should be able to make decisions in the bedroom without consulting him.

Men do become very tired of having to make all the decisions and come up with all the suggestions and ideas, whether in the bedroom or out of it. They usually ask the women in their lives for input but very often get little to none. It can get very frustrating if your partner answers every request for input with "I don't know—what do you want to do?"

I am very sympathetic with the reticence many women feel about suggesting something sexual. Many of us have invested a lifetime in hiding our sexual urges, submerging our sexual thoughts, lying about our level of sexual experience, and playing dumb when someone is sexually inappropriate. I can remember being completely ashamed when my husband told me how much he loved having sex with me because I loved sex so much. It was like he knew this deep, dark shameful secret about me. Somewhere along the line I was told that I would not be a good girl if I actually enjoyed sex. Even after years of being sexually active and years of marriage, those feelings persisted. I had to make a conscious effort to reject those feelings and claim my right to be a whole sexual being—not just available, but assertive.

The kind of role reversal I am talking about is not about catering to a man sexually. Catering to a man usually entails asking him what he wants and then giving it to him. I was never any good at that. I don't like to be told what to do. Rather I learned to tap into my own authentic sexual desire and channel that in ways that are also pleasing to my partners. I became skilled at sexual pleasuring of males and skilled at obtaining my own sexual satisfaction as well. If a man asked me to do this or that to him or for him, I would refuse. I preferred to initiate and direct the sexual scenario for his benefit as well as mine. That is true role reversal, because that is how most men make love to women. Men who are good lovers put a heavy emphasis on performing sexually for the female but not to the exclusion of their own sexual pleasure and preferences.

If you allow someone to direct you as if you were in a pornographic movie, you can expect similar results—bad acting and fake orgasms. The best sex comes from your heart and goes to your partner's heart. No one can direct authentic desire.

Role playing can also incorporate role reversal, but it certainly doesn't have to. A favorite male role-playing fantasy is "the secretary wants a raise from the boss." In this fantasy, I would be asked to play a client's secretary and to employ either sexual seduction or sexual submission to obtain an increase in pay. Interestingly, I have found that men who truly are powerful in their jobs prefer to give up control during their time off of work. And men who are still aspiring for more power on the job tend to have fantasies of being more powerful in the bedroom.

So "the secretary wants a raise from the boss" fantasy is preferred by men who don't own their own companies and have to take a certain amount of direction from their superiors. They are, in fact, reversing the day-to-day role that they play at work, while preserving the stereotypical roles between men and women. It was interesting for me to realize that although this fantasy conforms to gender roles, it is actually an attempt to counteract a perceived imbalance of power at work. I suspect that this same psychology might come to bear at home with their partners. In other words, it is possible that men who feel powerless at work might be more authoritarian in their personal relationships. Of course, these are generalizations, and there are always exceptions to the norm.

The men who wanted me to fulfill their fantasies about women forcing them to have sex were primarily CEOs, small business owners, and self-made millionaires/billionaires. This penchant for giving up control in fantasy as an antidote to having a great deal of control in daily life is an example of role playing that incorporates gender role reversal as well as reversal of the role played at work. I found it to be far more common than the fantasies of having control over a woman. But it is possible that this was simply an indication of the type of clients I tended to see, which were primarily the rich and powerful.

One thing is consistent, however. Almost all fantasy role play involves an exchange of power. So whether the man is in control or the woman is in control and regardless of why these particular roles are desired, the ultimate objective is to play with power. Some people may object to the whole concept as their sexual ideal is one of perfect equality and tender, nurturing love. There is nothing wrong with this type of sex either, but we should be free to experiment with new dynamics if we choose to. Nothing is wrong with power play as long as both participants are enjoying the dynamic.

In Chapter 26, I discuss how to role play in further detail. I also talk about women's sexual fantasies and how you and your partner can role play each other's fantasies. The primary purpose of Part 1, "Why Men Pay" has been to acquaint you with what I have learned about men while working as an escort. The remainder of this book will teach you how to seduce a man, how to initiate sex, and about specific sexual techniques to increase both his and your sexual satisfaction as well as providing insights into what it means to be a fully empowered sexual woman. But I'm getting ahead of myself. Read on to find out what "fair fighting" has to do with better orgasms!

6

Express Yourself for Better Sex

Many couples experience a dulling or slowing down of the sexual heat they initially felt for each other. Those first few months or years together can fulfill all our hottest and most romantic fantasies, but as time goes by we seem to lose something. What happens? Are we doomed to a boring sex life if we remain faithful and monogamous?

Although many experts will tell you that you need more variety in your sex life in order to keep it interesting, I disagree. Certainly, experimenting with new sexual techniques can be a very enlightening and erotic pursuit. But couples who do the same thing sexually for years can and do maintain their attraction for each other. Sexual technique and sexual variety are simply insufficient to create sexual heat all by themselves. In fact, singles who are having sex with multiple partners and are open to trying new things in bed also get bored with sex. Clearly, something else must constitute the essential ingredient when it comes to passion.

I have determined that suppressed emotions are what, in fact, diminish our capacity for sexual pleasure. Whenever you deny a feeling because you think it is inappropriate, you then have to bury it under mountains of shame and justification. In effect, you, turn the volume down on that part of you that feels. You might intend only to squelch the feelings that frighten you, such as anger or sadness. But in the bargain, you deaden all of your feelings. So your laughter feels a little more superficial, and your orgasms become less and less satisfying.

This is actually a pretty common pattern of events in long-term relationships. In the beginning, everything he does is so sexy, and you can't seem to keep your hands off each other. But then you have that horrible fight. It probably isn't the first time you had a fight. But it's the first time you didn't solve it. It was just too big for either one of you, and you went to your respective corners to sulk. After a while you convinced yourself it really wasn't worth fighting about after all, and you thought you could let go of your anger or hurt. You both agreed to forget about it and move on.

But, in fact, because you never really got to express your feelings instead of your rage, and because you never really felt heard instead of judged, and because you never got to the point where you experienced empathy for your partner—this emotional lump is now lodged in your heart, and it is blocking all of your feelings to a greater or lesser degree. On good days you tell yourself all is forgiven, and on bad days you wonder how you can take another 20 years of this.

Conflict is a normal part of all human interactions. Actually, it is a normal part of interaction for any living organism.

Knowing how to handle conflict and move through and past it as quickly as possible will not only keep your sex life on track for more pleasure and intimacy, but it will make for a happier life in general.

If you are like most couples, you treat your sex life as if it were not connected to all of this other stuff. But sex doesn't occur in a vacuum, and you can't expect your sex life to work unless your relationship is working. Occasionally I will meet a couple who flies in the face of this truth. They can't stand each other; they might even be on the verge of a break-up, but their hot sexual attraction for each other keeps them together. This is the exception, not the rule. For most of us, we have to keep our house in order on all levels if we want the sex to be great.

My husband and I had some of our hottest sex right after marriage counseling or private problem solving. After we had the chance to air our grievances and feel heard—truly heard, validated, and nurtured—it was automatic that we were attracted to each other and wanted to be sexually close. And because of all this hard emotional work, our sex life didn't just stay hot, it got hotter.

I have experienced a similar dynamic with my clients. For those clients who have chosen to spend their time with me revealing their vulnerabilities, the payoff has been incredible sex. Some men have just needed a good cry to get all the bottled up emotions out of their bodies. When that was accomplished, they could enjoy a deeper and more satisfying sexual union, as well as orgasms.

Part of my job as an escort or courtesan was to facilitate this expression of emotions from my clients. I would ask them probing questions about their lives, and most of them felt compelled to answer. I often heard them say that they couldn't believe they were sharing such deeply private feelings with me. And they were usually quite grateful to get these secrets and buried feelings off their chests. The nonjudgmental and safe atmosphere that I offered these men led them to talk about things they might fear to speak about with their partners or best friends. Of course, by sharing their intimate thoughts and feelings with me, they felt closer to me and safer with me. The end result was usually a deeply satisfying sexual experience.

Courtesans must refine the art of communication. Because she is being paid for her intellect and companionship as well as her time and sexual expertise, a courtesan must know how to relate to men on many different emotional, psychological, and intellectual levels.

There are many ways to describe healthy communication. Some call it "fair fighting," some call it "problem solving," and some refer to it as "active listening." But the bottom line is that all human interactions require successful communication to run satisfactorily.

Fair fighting can take a variety of forms, but it always entails abiding by a previously agreed upon set of rules. This is similar to the premise that governs most competitive sports, and it is a concept that most men take to very easily.

"No kitchen sinking" refers to the nasty habit many couples have of dragging up many incidents from the past when a conflict has arisen. This rule requires you to stay on the topic and in the present. It is considered "out of bounds" to overwhelm your partner with unresolved complaints from the past. Instead, you should both stick to the current issue.

Another fair fighting rule requires you to state your complaint in the "I feel" format. This is a communication style that refrains from attributing blame by keeping the focus on feelings instead of "facts." You might say something like this: "When you do _____, I feel _____ _____, I would like you to do _____ _____." Notice there are no judgments made about your partner's actions, and there is no defense made about your feelings. You are merely stating how you feel and what you want. Your partner has every right to refuse to change his behavior, but a proper response from him goes something like this: "I hear that you feel _____, when I do _____, and you would like me to do _____. Have I heard you correctly?" If he has replayed your statements correctly, then he can move on to validating your feelings and expressing whether he is open to changing his behavior.

Believe it or not, whether your partner is willing to change his behavior or not, you will still benefit from expressing your feelings and having them validated. In fact, you may find that the two of you feel closer and warmer about each other despite the fact that you may not agree on a given course of action. Validating another's feelings involves active listening, which requires you to stop thinking about what you are going to say next and truly listen to your partner.

Active listening leads to empathy, which involves sharing the feelings of others. If you actively listen to your partner, and your partner states his feelings without accusing or blaming you, empathy will almost always result. And when you feel empathy for another person, it is easy to validate his feelings. When you validate feelings, you let the other person know that you not only understand his feelings but you feel compassion for him. Validation does not mean that you have agreed to any specific course of action or change in behavior. It is simply an empathic action that will bring you closer to each other regardless of whether you are able to agree on what to do. This increased emotional intimacy has an amazing effect on physical intimacy. After doing the emotional work of the relationship, you may actually feel as if your love life has been taken to a new high that exceeds your wildest expectations!

The formula that follows can assist you in the emotional work of your relationship and has a very high level of success for most couples. Most men are more open to the information and the resulting change in behavior if you present it as a formula:

Expression of Feelings (without Blaming) → Active Listening → Empathy → Validation of Feelings → Improved Intimacy → Better Sex

I know you can create this in your own life. But it does require a little courage. Every one of us lives in fear of our own thoughts and emotions. Getting past that fear and taking the risk of confiding in a trustworthy person is an important step in lowering our defenses so that we are open to pleasure—the pleasure of emotions such as laughter and love and the pleasure of sensuality and sex.

7

Sexy Is as Sexy Does

Before I became an escort, I had an attitude about my body and myself that was pretty typical of women. I always felt like I needed to lose more weight no matter how thin I was. I always felt inferior to the women on TV and in the magazines. I was painfully aware of those parts of my body that I wanted to change.

Sometimes I became so distracted by what I imagined I looked like that I couldn't even enjoy sex. I might obsess over the size and shape of my thighs or what my face would look like if I dared to grimace during a moment of sexual pleasure. I would worry about sweating too much or being in positions that were less than flattering. And I certainly did not want to appear to enjoy sex "too much" lest my male partner conclude that I was some kind of slut. Because I was so busy critiquing and censoring myself, sex was not something I enjoyed all that much.

The first time I saw myself having sex on film, many of my previous fears faded. I realized that many of the things I imagined grotesque about myself simply did not exist. You may not be ready to make a home movie, but you can take some steps to learn to appreciate yourself as a sexy woman.

Today, our culture is completely obsessed with the exterior. We focus on how the outside body looks to the exclusion of some factors that used to be considered more sexually arousing. For instance, if Marilyn Monroe were alive today, she would be mercilessly picked apart by the press for being "chunky," and then we fans would be denied the exquisite intoxication of her sexy voice, mannerisms, and walk. Similarly, a beauty like Lauren Bacall, whose sultry voice and sexy stroll made many weak in the knees, might be dismissed as too skinny and flat-chested before she could ever rise to fame.

So many of today's so-called sex symbols leave me feeling little that could be mistaken for sexual arousal. A firm round bottom and rock hard abs are not sexy all by themselves. Sexy is as sexy does. And many "perfect" beauties simply do not possess sex appeal. We know this intuitively and usually experience it with great confusion. How can that person look so good but be so unappealing? It happens because sex appeal is far more complex than the right diet or exercise regimen or even the "perfect" genetic code.

Maybe you have noticed the opposite as well—a person who seems to be a little gawky or unremarkable in appearance but nevertheless possesses a magnetism that defies logic. You might have spent some time trying to figure out what it is about that person that makes him or her so attractive. If you are like me, you probably could never put it into words. They simply are sexy.

I believe that almost all people look very sexy when they are in the throes of authentic sensual delight. It cannot be faked or put on for an audience. Those performances can be humorous but rarely sexy. However, if an individual comes from their core and expresses their innermost joy and desire devoid of any self-consciousness, then true beauty is the result.

Most women tend to have a negative and rather distorted view of what they look like naked. Many women don't like what they see when they stand naked in front of a mirror. Some women are so embarrassed they won't even let their husbands or boyfriends see them naked with the lights on. Because most of us have been programmed to feel inadequate by media messages, you have to take a proactive approach to get past that negativity and learn to feel sexy!

While I was learning to get past my own low self-esteem, I used props to bolster my confidence. Lingerie and high heels are designed to enhance a woman's best assets. You never see competitors for the Miss America crown parade barefoot during the swimsuit competition. Instead, they wear high heels because high-heeled shoes tilt the legs and butt into a more flattering configuration. Likewise, push-up bras accentuate the bust line and G-strings make any figure look better.

I used to dress up and practice my walk and poses in front of a full-length mirror. Then I had photos taken by a professional photographer. I needed the photos for advertising, but many women have taken advantage of the confidence booster that boudoir photography can offer. After you see yourself looking sexy in a photo, you can replace any negative image that you carry in your head with real photos of yourself. It is one way to reprogram a low sense of self.

Sex appeal has a synergistic effect, so that the <u>more sexy you feel,</u> the more sexy you are perceived to be by your partner. Conversely, the more sexy he thinks you are, the more sexy you feel. An empowered approach is to get things started by

improving the way you feel about yourself. Don't wait for him
to change his mind. Change it for him. The best way to do that
is to change your opinion of yourself.

After I began to believe that I was sexy, things like lingerie
and footwear mattered less. I started to simply be sexy no
matter what I was wearing (or not wearing). I learned to carry
myself with confidence, and my clients believed me to be
sexy, too. Confidence, body confidence in particular, cannot be
underestimated. If I have to pick one thing that communicates
sexiness more than anything else, it is confidence.

From confidence you get permission to be shameless. If you
feel ashamed of how you look, of being naked, or of being
sexual, that shame will be communicated in everything you
do. Shame is the opposite of sexy. Unfortunately, we women
receive a lot of messages that encourage us to feel shame about
our sexuality as well as our bodies. Not only does that shame
make us feel self-conscious about our appearance, it reduces
our capacity to enjoy sex.

Sex requires us to let go, stop thinking, start feeling, and
get swept away by our passions. Believe it or not, meditation
can actually help. In meditation you learn to turn off your
thoughts and simply be. This can be facilitated with breathing
exercises. It just so happens that being able to turn off your
thoughts and breathe freely are also very important ingredients
to great sex. So if you are having trouble letting go and enjoying sex, you might consider a meditation class as one way to
enhance your sex life.

Truly good sex also requires us to step out of that part of
our brain that handles formulas and technical information. This
other side of the equation is the domain of intuition. When I

first began my career as an escort, I didn't know how to use my intuition. Fortunately, I had a mentor, and she taught me to tap into my intuition. It seemed like so much nonsense at first, but I watched her effectively screen potential clients over the phone by using a combination of experience and intuition. I watched and listened as she read situations accurately. She was even able to use her intuition accurately when having sex with men she knew little about. It was amazing to me how incredibly accurate her intuition could be.

So I set aside my skepticism and gave my own intuition a chance to guide me. It was difficult at first to tell the difference between the logical voices in my head and the guidance my intuition was offering me. But in time, I came to know the difference.

As I practiced emptying my mind of the loud chatter of logic and letting those quiet feelings pull me in one direction or another, I began to enjoy smoother interactions with others, which included a more satisfying sexual experience. Letting go of my logic not only allowed my intuition to guide me, but it opened the door to spontaneity and passion.

Another way you can break free from old patterns of self-consciousness and shame is by employing humor. We don't usually associate being funny with being sexy, but I have found that a playful approach to sex can go a long way to creating an improved sex life. I used jokes and playfulness on a regular basis to help my clients get past their own low self-esteem and self-consciousness so they could enjoy sex. Too many men suffer from performance anxiety and, therefore, take sex way too seriously. I envisioned one of my roles as someone who wanted to heal and help men's sexual expression, and a very vital part of that role incorporated humor.

But humor also helped me to let go of my inhibitions during sex. Some appropriate moments to use humor include any unintended results, such as fumbling while disrobing or having a condom fly out of your hands. I even used humor when a man lost his erection. This was actually a very effective way to bring the erection back! Simply saying something silly like "is *he* feeling shy today?" while pointing at his limp penis was often all that was required to allow the body's natural sexual response to take over. The man might laugh or smirk, but the end result was that he stopped thinking about his erection and relaxed long enough to allow his penis to function.

Too many times both men and women get so preoccupied with their self-conscious thoughts that their genitals don't get a chance to operate normally. So if you feel tense or stressed or you sense uncomfortable feelings on the part of your partner, find a reason to laugh. For instance, you can allow yourself to laugh if air escapes from your vagina during sex or if the motion of your two sweaty bodies produces fartlike noises. Give yourself and your partner permission to approach sex with a sense of humor. It really is a very freeing feeling. And it is often the best cure for less-than-optimum sexual response in both men and women.

Whether you are attempting to find your soul mate, foster new friendships, or keep the fires of an existing relationship burning bright, you will find the following 10 tips quite helpful. In fact, these principles can help you in other areas of your life as well, such as in your emotional well-being and career aspirations. Obviously, some tips are only pertinent to your sex life, such as how well you clean your genitals, but most of what makes us sexually attractive also makes us socially attractive.

1. Get Clean. In addition to bathing regularly, it is especially important to have clean genitals, a clean rectum (baby wipes come in handy for this), and sweet smelling breath (watch your blood sugar, as going without food for long periods of time can cause a foul odor). Skip the cologne or perfume, or use it sparingly, if you must wear it.

2. Be Attentive. Everyone wants to feel special, and the best way to make someone feel special is to listen attentively. Don't just nod your head and say "uh huh." Make mental notes about the things that they indicate are the most important to them and be sure to mention these things at a later date. Then your special someone will know they were important enough for you to pay attention. That fact alone will make you incredibly attractive.

3. Be Interesting. Try to become the person with whom you want to be. If your life is full and interesting to you, you will attract a partner, and even friends, more easily. No one wants to be around a bore, so make sure that you don't bore yourself. If you like being with you, chances are more than a few other people will feel the same way.

4. Be Informed. Listen to the news, read the paper, research a favorite topic. Knowing what is going on in the world (current affairs), as well as having some historical perspective (history, the arts, culture), not only makes you a more attractive guest at parties but ensures that you will not come across as "out of date" or "dull." As long as you don't dominate conversations with unwanted information or expose your education with an attitude of superiority, being knowledgeable is an asset in any social situation. An added benefit is that you are capable of conversing with and, therefore, bonding with a broader range of individuals. Of course, this only makes you more attractive to the opposite sex.

5. Become Experienced. Experience is similar to education. You don't want to beat people over the head with how experienced you are, but you do want to make sure that you are experienced in a variety of pursuits. Being good in bed is, of course, a must, but you should also know how to engage in a variety of sports and/or games. You don't want to beg off when the fun starts because you "don't know how." If you have a favorite sport or hobby, it may make for an ideal activity to share with someone you love or are just getting to know. Make sure that you have several interests; if your partner finds one activity insufferable, they will hopefully enjoy another of your interests.

6. Be Adventurous. No one likes a coward or a show-off. Be sure to avoid either extreme while cultivating your sense of adventure. Don't be foolhardy, but take a few risks and enjoy life! Your bravery will excite and inspire others, as well as add to your personal sense of fulfillment.

7. Be Sensuous. Develop an intimate relationship with your own body. Take up dancing, start working out, and masturbate. Relate to the world with all of your senses. Slow down to enjoy the taste of good food and savor the colors and smells at your table. Look up and truly see the sky. Are there clouds? What shapes are they? Is the sun setting? How many colors can you count? Is there a full moon? What shapes do you think the stars create? Let go and feel the music vibrate into your very bones. Breathe deeply and let the fullness of being alive and made of flesh infect you with its sheer joy!

8. Be Confident. High self-esteem, which is nothing like pride, is very attractive. Everyone wants to be around people who are sure of themselves and in charge of their own lives. It is only when people lack true confidence and self-esteem that they attempt to control others. Confidence means you are responsible for yourself, and you never try to dominate others. True confidence is similar to boundaries in that it creates safety and security for those around you. You can be trusted. As a result, many people will seek your counsel when you are confident, thereby putting you in a leadership role. A confident person never violates that trust.

9. Be Assertive. Contrary to popular thinking, assertiveness has nothing to do with aggressiveness. As a matter of fact, they are polar opposites. If you can assert your boundaries in a healthy manner, you will create an atmosphere of safety for your prospective partner. He won't be guessing at your meaning, intentions, desires, or thoughts. Knowing the rules makes for a level of comfort and security that invites emotional intimacy.

10. Be Loving. Care about others regardless of what may or may not be in it for you. When you attempt to manipulate people, places, or things for your own satisfaction, it will eventually backfire. The very things you want will slip through your hands like sand. The only way to attract what you want is to let it go. So don't be stingy or conniving with your affection. Give your love freely in the context of appropriate boundaries, and you will find you have become simply irresistible!

8

Caring for Your Temple

I learned to be an escort from another escort. She was a beautiful woman who knew how to take care of herself. At first, her capacity for pampering herself seemed over-indulgent and decadent to me. But after I had been an escort for a few months, I changed my tune. I realized rather quickly that the only way to feel sexy and to be sexy is to treat yourself like the sexiest woman alive!

You have no doubt heard the saying "your body is your temple." This admonition is usually used to warn us against eating inappropriate foods, smoking, drinking too much, and so on. In fact, one's health is very important when it comes to sex. Illness, depression, fatigue, and hormonal irregularities can have a disastrous effect on one's sex life. But I prefer a more positive spin on this old adage. Rather than focus on all the things you should not do, I prefer to talk about all the things you can do to make yourself feel like a queen or a priestess!

Pampering and self-care can take the form of a regular beauty regimen, such as having your hair and nails done. It can also include professional massage, facials, paraffin treatments (your hands and feet are dipped in hot wax that is peeled off after it cools leaving your skin soft—very pleasurable), endermologie (a type of massage that claims to reduce cellulite—it does so temporarily but more importantly, it feels good!), body wraps and scrubs, and hydrotherapy (mineral baths). Many of these services are offered at day spas. Try meeting a girlfriend for a light lunch and gossip and then spend the rest of the afternoon pampering yourselves with a multitude of treatments.

Notice when I suggest pampering and self-care, I am not referring to something as drastic as plastic surgery. In fact, the kind of pampering I am suggesting is just the opposite of makeovers, extreme or otherwise. A makeover suggests that you are not enough, and you require some sort of change to be acceptable. I am referring to things that make you feel good and that communicate to yourself that you are worthy of special attention. The kind of pampering that escorts engage in is about rejuvenating our bodies and our spirits so we feel refreshed. If we feel good, we are able to project that inner feeling of bliss into everything we do. And that makes us sexually attractive to others.

Of course, most escorts also spend a great deal of time and effort on perfecting their appearance. I follow a regimen that is both about enhancing my sexual attractiveness as well as making me feel pampered and sexy.

Not only is exercise an integral contribution to my emotional well-being, physical health, and sexual vitality, but because sex is a physical activity, it is enhanced when I am limber and when my heart and lungs function properly. Regular exercise improves your cardiovascular health to accommodate great sex! Exercise also releases endorphins and testosterone: endorphins are hormones that improve your mood and reduce chronic pain, and testosterone actually boosts your sex drive.

You should never start a new exercise program without first consulting with your doctor to make sure that you don't have any serious health problems which might limit your ability to safely engage in certain physical exertion. As long as you have a clean bill of health, you can engage in a variety of physical activities that will only improve your sex life in the long run. But even if your doctor imposes limitations on the exercise you can engage in, he or she will no doubt prescribe some type of physical activity. It is important that you do what you can.

Personally, I love weight lifting. It tones and shapes muscles so that they have a pleasing and sensuous look. But even more pertinent to your sex life is the fact that a firm body feels good to both you and your sexual partner. If you work with heavy weights, you can add size to a particular muscle group if you so desire. But it is entirely possible to work with weights without adding size. All you have to do is decrease the amount of weight you lift or push and increase the number of times you move that weight (repetitions). If you are curious about weight lifting, be sure to get a trainer to work with at least in the beginning. Any specialized physical activity requires training to reduce your chances of injury. And some people find that a trainer keeps them motivated.

Many people love yoga or Pilates, which are very different types of exercise and yet they both improve your strength, muscle tone, and flexibility. Many gyms and clubs offer classes in both. There are also cardiovascular classes such as aerobics, spin, and step. You might have fun taking an introductory class in each until you find the one that works best for you. Who knows, you may decide to take up several!

While you are designing your personal exercise routine, don't forget to exercise the most important muscle for your sex life: your PC (pubococcygeus) muscle. This is a group of muscles that surround your genitals and support your pelvic floor. Both men and women have this muscle, which helps us control urination. If you can start and stop your flow of urine, you know how to use your PC muscle. If you exercise this muscle, you can improve your sex life on many levels.

One way to exercise this muscle is by having frequent sexual intercourse. Although popular myth would tell you otherwise, a woman who has lots of sex will actually end up with a tighter and firmer vaginal tract than if she was not using those muscles. Strong PC muscles enhance vaginal orgasms, enjoyment of the G-spot, and female ejaculations. It can also increase a man's sexual pleasure during intercourse because the woman can literally squeeze his penis with her vagina.

You can exercise this muscle in other ways. You can practice contracting and relaxing your PC muscle while you are sitting in traffic in your car or sitting at your computer at work! Some brave souls even exercise their PC muscles while in line at the bank or grocery store. If you want to build even more muscle tone, you can purchase barbells for the vagina. This unique exercise equipment is available from online sources such as Good Vibrations (www.goodvibes.com).

If you start exercising on a regular basis, you will no doubt find yourself craving a massage. Exercise and massage are made for each other! Like exercise, massage is a wonderful way to reduce your stress level. And massage gives you permission to experience pleasure and pampering, which can lead to more enjoyable sex. Massage requires that you submit to being the center of attention; you cannot reciprocate. That hour or two is just for you.

My favorite types of massage include Shiatsu (a traditional hands-on Japanese healing art), deep tissue (a massage technique that focuses on the deeper layers of muscle tissue), acupressure (an ancient Chinese healing method that involves applying pressure to certain meridian points on the body), Myofascial (a highly interactive stretching technique), and hot rock massage (heated stones are applied to the body and used to massage muscle). Another popular form of massage is Swedish. Swedish techniques include long strokes, kneading, friction, tapping, percussion, vibration, effleurage (rhythmic stroking), and shaking motions.

The most extravagant massage experience I ever had was called a symphonic massage because it required two massage therapists. It was terribly expensive, and I could not have justified the cost, so I am grateful that a client treated me to it. For one hour and a half, *two* men gave me a sports massage (a technique that involves a blend of traditional Swedish Massage and Shiatsu specifically designed to treat professional athletes) *simultaneously*! Four hands kneading all the day's tensions from my muscles were utterly exquisite! They ended the massage with an oatmeal scrub for my feet. When it was over, I was putty and could scarcely remember what day it was.

It is also a wonderful gift to yourself to ask your partner to give you a massage. Depending upon your mood, you may want to clarify with him that you just want a massage—not sex. This may be easier said than done if your partner finds you irresistible. But impress upon him the importance of your being able to trust him to refrain from sexual touching unless you have invited it. You can agree to give him a "no strings-attached" massage afterward or on another day. Many men actually find this a very attractive offer. Some of my clients found the massage that I provided so intoxicating and relaxing they decided to forgo sex and just enjoy the release of days or weeks of stress. Most of us have far more stress in our bodies than we are aware of, and massage can feel almost as good as sex!

Beauty may seem to be the province of women, but if you are like me, you would be surprised to find out how many men notice the little details in women's personal grooming. Some men always notice the hands; some are more inclined to appreciate an excellent pedicure; and others care more about soft skin, but each man is usually fond of a particular form of female grooming. Many men have particular fetishes for the presence or absence of body hair on a woman. Most men prefer shaved legs and underarms, but this preference is by no means universal. In fact there are entire websites and magazines devoted to men who have a fetish for hirsute (hairy) women.

It is important that you groom yourself in a manner that suits your preferences. If you begin to cater to the expectations of your man or society, you will also be on the road to undermining your sense of individuality, which has a direct effect on your level of confidence. And remember, nothing is as sexy as confidence. Therefore, when in doubt, do what feels most comfortable to you.

When I became an escort, I immediately modified my personal grooming habits. For instance, before I might have just shaved the sides of my pubic hair during bikini season.

Suddenly this part of my anatomy seemed far more important to me, and I wanted it to be the very best it could be, so I attended to it in a variety of ways. First, I made sure my vulva was always impeccably clean. The people who manufacture douches and feminine hygiene products would like you to think this can only be accomplished by using their products. But in fact, I have learned that douching and using chemicals only produces more problems with odor and hygiene in the long run.

Douching depletes the vagina of the healthy bacteria that keep it smelling fresh naturally. So if you get into the habit of douching frequently, you will have to douche indefinitely. It is much better for your health as well as your hygiene if you eat right, because a healthy body translates to a healthy vagina. You can supplement the bacteria that maintain a pleasant vaginal aroma by taking probiotics (available at your health store in a variety of forms) orally and/or inserting them as a vaginal suppository. If you have enough of the good bacteria, you will be healthier, and you will smell and taste divine.

Washing is very important, too, but in most cases you need to clean only the outside genitals, paying close attention to wash your clitoris and between your labia. Water is enough, but you can also use a little mild soap if you prefer. Smegma (a protective coating and lubricant for the glans of the clitoris or the penis) does collect under the clitoral hood just as it does under the foreskin of an intact penis, so if you don't wash every day, you may notice some odor there. Simple hygiene can rectify this, but some odors are more indicative of systemic health problems. If you experience an unpleasant odor and/or discharge from your vagina, be sure to see a doctor immediately.

Occasionally you may have to douche due to an overgrowth of the wrong kind of bacteria and/or fungus, but even then I recommend you stay away from the commercial douches. Homemade douches of vinegar or yogurt work much better, and you can find a variety of recipes on the Internet. Again, make sure that you do this only once in a while. Your objective should be to maintain your health so that douching is something you do only a couple times a year (certainly never more than once a month). I have found that probiotics also ward off yeast infections, so I take them on a daily basis. Yeast infections are caused by a species of fungus called *Candida albicans*. Like all yeasts, *Candida albicans* loves sugar, so during times of stress or if I have consumed more sugar than usual, I will double up on my probiotics to assist my vagina in maintaining a healthy bacterial balance.

Obviously, a healthy vulva is a sexy vulva, but there are some cosmetic things you can do to amplify the sex appeal of your genitals. You may like to try shaving or waxing your pubic hair. Some women shave or wax just enough to facilitate wearing a bikini. However, others find that cutting the pubic hair very short or shaving it off completely can make sex more pleasurable and/or exciting for both her and her man.

I prefer to keep my pubic hair a thin line of short hair in front and completely shaved in back. Some people playfully refer to this particular form of pubic grooming as a "landing strip," which is not to be confused with the Brazilian bikini wax, which removes all of the hair in back and most or all of the hair in front. A Brazilian can entail a landing strip, a triangle, or nothing at all in front. Technically, I do wear one type of Brazilian, but I prefer to use a combination of shaving, trimming, and epilating (most of these devices remove hair by pulling it up by the roots, similar to waxing) rather than getting a wax. Some women also use depilatories (chemicals that dissolve the hair) or seek permanent hair removal through laser treatments.

If you would rather accentuate your pubic hair than remove it, you can also try coloring it. The manufacturers of hair coloring agents as well as most medical professionals do not recommend that you apply any colorant to your pubic hair. The vulva consists of very sensitive tissues that can easily be irritated by harsh chemicals. However, some people do it anyway. I did. I learned how from my girlfriend. The process required that I use gobs of petroleum jelly on my labia to protect it from any hair dye that might drip onto it. I was very careful and quite pleased with the results. No matter what color the hair on my head was, I could match that color "down below."

If you do decide to try dying your pubic hair, you should be forewarned that you do so at your own risk. Again, it is not the proper use of hair-coloring agents. And second, you should make sure you apply the hair color only to the top front portion of your pubic hair. So you will need to shave or wax the hair surrounding your vagina if you don't want to be two-toned. Because most pubic hair is thicker and coarser than the hair on our heads, you may find that dyes made for beards work better. You can also find some spas and salons that will color your pubic hair for you, although they don't usually advertise the service.

Of course, there are many other parts of your body that you may choose to groom one way or another. As women, we are faced with myriad options including hair color and style, how to shape our eyebrows, whether and how to wear makeup, and whether we choose to shave our legs. If we do want to take the hair off our legs, we have just as many options as we did when it came to grooming our vulvas, including waxes, depilatories, razors, epilators, or laser treatments. You may choose to tan or avoid the sun for health reasons. If you still want a bronze glow, you can use self-tanners for some harmless skin color. And, of course, there are many options available for obtaining whiter teeth. You can buy over-the-counter concoctions or pay hundreds of dollars for a dentist to bleach your teeth with a laser light beam. I chose the latter.

Some women love long fingernails, and others like to keep them short and practical. Regardless of your personal style, it will go a long way toward helping you feel sexy if you do adopt a regular grooming schedule. Rather than saving a manicure or pedicure for special occasions, you may choose to make this a weekly or monthly ritual. I like to have my toenails perfectly trimmed and painted all year long. Even though the public will not see my toes in the winter, my lover will. And I want to make sure I feel completely attractive and sexy when I take my shoes off. Whether you paint your toenails or not, you certainly don't need your feet to be anything less than attractive and sensuous, however you define that. The same applies to your hands. Your fingertips and hands play a very important role during sex!

Your skin is also extremely important during sex, so you will want to make sure that it is as soft and sensuous as possible. I use a loofah sponge (the fibrous portion of a gourd) all over my body every time I shower. You can also buy exfoliating gloves that work very well to scrub off the dead skin that can cause roughness. Exfoliation is the removal of the dead layer of cells that often covers our skin. Problem spots are the elbows, knees, and feet, so pay special attention to them. After using a loofah or even a washcloth while I am bathing or showering, I like to follow up with an exfoliating body lotion. Many of these lotions are on the market, and they not only moisturize your skin like regular lotion, but actually smooth and soften the surface of your skin by exfoliation. You can find face creams that contain exfoliating ingredients as well, and I highly recommend them.

Courtesans are expected to blend with the conservative community their clients frequent, and with that comes certain expectations in personal grooming as well as clothing. I often dressed more conservatively when I was boarding an airplane to meet a gentleman for a rendezvous than I did in my day-to-day life. I might wear a miniskirt to a party with my personal friends, but I would rarely find a miniskirt appropriate when with a client. I even made sure my fingernails were short to medium and clear or neutral in color. I would never wear acrylic nails when escorting a conservative man. My blonde hair was almost too blonde for the job. In fact, one client refused to take me on a trip to a Midwest town because my hair was too blonde for the locale. He said I would stand out and draw too much attention. He preferred to travel with me on the West Coast where blondes abound.

Obviously, since I was getting paid, I had to conform to the dress code for my job. I certainly would not think it appropriate for a woman to modify her appearance or her clothing for her partner. However, this anecdote does highlight how important clothing and grooming can be to some men. It also serves as a reminder that our appearance is often a way to communicate social status or membership to others. For me, that can be a double-edged sword. I don't particularly care for judging people by their exteriors, and yet we all do it to a greater or lesser degree.

It can be difficult to sort out which of our choices is a personal choice and which is dictated by cultural norms, peer pressure, or our own low self-esteem. I would just ask you to remember to have fun when it comes to caring for your temple. This is about helping you feel good. It is not about what others think about you. It goes back to an old truth: it is not so much what you do but why you do it.

9

Setting the Mood

In college, you were likely to find naked pictures of men adorning my dormitory room. As an escort, I continued this tradition with naked pictures of women on the walls of my "office." I thought the visual stimulation would be an aphrodisiac for my clients. Many men were quite thrilled to meet a woman who wasn't afraid of pornographic images. But my clientele improved a hundred percent when a friend gave my apartment a face lift.

She was a woman gifted with an exquisite sense of style, and she transformed my den of carnal pleasures into a sensual retreat that men never wanted to leave. Frankly, the place was so inviting, I never wanted to leave. When a man walked over the threshold, his senses were engaged immediately. Not only would I be seductively attired in fine lingerie; the entire room beckoned him to enter.

Aromatherapy candles would flicker from every corner of the room, casting a romantic glow and mysterious shadows. The earthy fragrances of cedar wood, sandalwood, sage, and lavender would travel on subtle smoke curls intoxicating the moment. Heavy curtains made of gold fabric embossed with barely visible outlines of flowers and leaves intercepted the sunlight to preserve the eroticism of the candlelight and tinge it with a subtle hint of gold hues. The faint trickle of water bubbled from two small water fountains strategically placed near the four-poster bed and the massage table. The mood was completed with sensual music—either classical, such as Mozart or Beethoven, or new age albums by artists such as Enya, Enigma, or Yanni.

But there was no reason to stop there. And so I didn't. Not only did I want to arouse the senses of smell, sight, and sound—but also the senses of touch and taste. Offering a beverage can be a polite and effective way to arouse the sense of taste. Something that bubbles like champagne or sparkling water not only tastes good but tickles the taste buds for an added erotic dimension. Light fare such as fresh fruit can also serve as a sensuous prelude. There is something quite exquisite about hand-feeding your lover a chocolate-covered strawberry.

Skin that is caressed by expensive sheets with a thread count over 300 is skin that feels pampered. Even the roughest manly man can tell the difference. He may not know a thing about sheets or thread count, but his skin can't help but respond favorably to the touch of fine sheets. It's best to stick to white or subtle pastels. Most men do not care for loud colors or bold prints when it comes to bedding. You want to select something that is at once romantic and gender-neutral. My sheets were white, off-white, mint, and light gold, embossed with the faint outline of leaves. They not only looked great, they felt good. If you have to choose between the way the sheets look and the way they feel, it's best to buy the sheets that feel good.

I should mention here that skimping on the furniture and the décor of your bedroom is not a good idea if you intend to share many romantic moments there. Certainly, lovemaking can take place in other rooms in the house, but it's nice to have at least one room that is devoted to eroticism and romance. Your bed should be comfortable, roomy, and inviting. Investing in a good mattress and a luxurious headboard can do wonders to revive your love life. Keep in mind that you are shopping for two, so don't transform the bedroom into something all your girlfriends will admire.

You want to be careful to pick colors and fabrics with which your man will feel comfortable. Although most men will say they don't care about household decorating, they usually only say this to avoid conflict. In my experience, the décor of my boudoir was of great interest to the men I saw. If the ambiance resonated with them, they were tempted to stay longer. In fact, one client paid to redecorate and refurnish my apartment because he intended to spend a lot of time there, and he wanted to surround himself with opulence.

Although it is possible to design a room that is enticing to most men, I found that men's preferences in lingerie were extremely diverse and rather entrenched. If he liked garters and stockings, he didn't care for bare skin. If he preferred bare skin, he found lingerie to be an annoying obstacle. Men who liked fetish heels had nothing in common with men who had a thing for the classic pump. Some men loved the slutty look, and others were repulsed by it. A surprising number of men knew more about women's lingerie than I did, having become expert shoppers in the genre over the years while obtaining gifts for the women in their lives. Fortunately for me, these men taught me a lot about fine lingerie, which became my preference.

If you are not sure what your man likes in the way of lingerie, you can do a little experiment. Present him with several photos from catalogs for various manufacturers of women's lingerie and let him pick his favorites. Make sure you select photos that represent a variety of styles, colors, and prices. You may be surprised to find out that he has far more specific tastes in women's lingerie than you ever imagined. Most men do. They have been looking at photos of women in lingerie for years, and they know what they like. Of course, some men get confused and can't tell whether they like the photo because of the woman in the lingerie or the lingerie itself. In some cases, you can weed out the "choices" that have more to do with the model than the clothes by showing him a variety of outfits modeled by one woman.

Of course, if your budget can support it, you may choose to be the model. If you can afford to buy a variety of lingerie that you enjoy and then model it for him, you will not only develop a sense of what he prefers, but you may arouse his appreciation for styles he didn't think he liked. Regardless of what he likes or doesn't like, you can't go wrong when you try on lingerie for your man. Half the fun for him will be how special he feels when you go to the trouble to dress up for him and ask him what he likes. Half the fun for you will be all the attention he will be paying to you while you are dressing up in sexy clothes. And, if your man turns out to be that rare breed that hates lingerie, then hopefully he will have fun ripping it off of you!

Great sex is not just about props and technique. I will say that several times in this book. It is vital that you understand that most great sex begins in the brain. If you are tired or distracted, you won't feel that sexy. If you are angry at your partner, it is going to be difficult to get "into the mood" no matter how much planning and preparation you have expended in setting a mood in your bedroom. So *your* mood is the most important part of the equation.

First, I recommend getting to the bottom of your fatigue, anger, or any other emotions you may be experiencing. Long-term happiness and sexual satisfaction depend upon it. But if you are already working on your "issues" and you want some time off in the form of fantastic sex, there are ways to put these thoughts and feelings aside temporarily.

I have found deep-breathing exercises very helpful in getting me back into my body and focused on sensation instead of thought. I breathe in through my nose, hold my breath for just a couple seconds, and then let it out through my mouth. As I expel my breath I sometimes make a noise such as a sigh or moan. This helps me to relax and release some emotions as well.

Stretching is a great thing to do before sex, too. Be careful not to bounce when you stretch. Just extend yourself as far as is comfortable and hold that position until the count of 20. Slow gentle movements are best when you stretch. This will make you feel more limber and alive and ready for physical activity (which sex is). It will also serve to get you out of your head and into your body.

Some people love to work out before sex. Some exercise can be great to raise your testosterone levels (the hormone that gives you a sex drive), and it also gets you breathing. As long as you don't work out too hard (you want to save some energy for lovemaking), exercise can be a wonderful way to make you feel sexy and ready for love!

Others prefer a more sedate approach to seduction. Romantic bubble baths are wonderful for this. Soaking in a hot tub alone or with your partner are options you might consider. Whether you are alone or with him, candlelight and a favorite beverage are guaranteed to make you feel more relaxed and sensuous. If you invite him into the tub with you, you may not make it out of the water!

Mutual massage is another method for moving your attention away from the cares of the day and toward your goal of sexual bliss. After you have set the mood in your bedroom (or whatever room you have chosen for your rendezvous), you can begin by exchanging body rubs. Many sensuous oils and lotions are designed just for such occasions.

As you can see, a lot of planning goes into exquisite sex. I don't wish to set yet another benchmark for you to aspire to. Rather, I hope you will give yourself permission to have fun experimenting until you find your personal favorites. The idea is not to give you more work to do, but hopefully to give you permission to approach sex as a very important, special, and fun part of your life. Enjoy!

10

Using Your Mind to Arouse

My early ads as an escort read something like this:

Veronica Monet—Voluptuous, Sensual, and Sincere Strawberry Blonde with Big Green Eyes. 36C-25-36. Call 415-xxx-xxxx.

Then I lost 10 pounds and began lifting weights. The ads changed to this:

Veronica Monet—Healthy Hard Body has Hugs for You— Call for the TLC you deserve! 415-xxx-xxxx.

After I had figured out that the best clients were more interested in my brain than my body, I advertised as follows:

International Escort and Television Personality—Veronica Monet—I love stimulating conversation whether it's over a five-course meal at an expensive restaurant or a bottle of Evian in your hotel room. I am an excellent conversationalist and a published writer. Look for me on upcoming television shows such as A&E's Love Chronicles.

It is important to me that you receive more than you are used to during our time together. That may translate into a variety of things including but not limited to a meaningful and heart-felt connection or erotic splendors yet unknown. Together we will create an encounter that suits your needs as well as your desires. Contact: 1-888-xxx-xxxx.

Of course, my advertising changed as I did, and with those changes came a difference in the kind of men that called me. Or perhaps the men were the same, but their interactions with me were different. I can think of several instances in which the latter is true, because I had many of the same clients for more than a decade. Our time together took on a depth that could only lead to a heightened sense of fulfillment, both emotionally as well as sexually.

What I didn't understand in the beginning is that men are cerebral creatures. Contrary to popular humor, men are for the most part thinking individuals and as such truly appreciate intellectual stimulation. In fact, the early courtesans predicated their relationships with men almost exclusively upon intellectual stimulation. It was apparently common knowledge a few hundred years ago that the biggest sex organ in humans is the brain!

The courtesans of old knew that men gravitated to them because they were educated, accomplished, and not the least bit shy about showing their intelligence. Courtesans were renowned for expressing themselves plainly and unapologetically—so much so that they often came across as argumentative and even hotheaded. Yet the men were attracted to them, not despite their aggressive intellect and verbal fencing skills, but precisely because they were not docile or agreeable. Apparently, the sexual libido is aroused by a certain amount of conflict.

This is perhaps more apparent in the way that physical activity like sports and exercise boosts the testosterone levels in both males and females. Have you ever engaged in a little playful "rough-housing" only to find it followed by intense sexual desire? You see such scenarios in movies all the time: the boy and girl are wrestling either playfully or in earnest and then suddenly the humor or anger turns to sexual passion. This can seem contrived in the movies, but it neverthe-less exemplifies a rather common occurrence in real life.

Some people are familiar with something known as "make-up sex." A couple has a fight, and after they resolve the conflict they find themselves attracted to each other again. The result-ing sex is often more intense than it was before the conflict. This can be a very hot part of one's sex life, but it is not the same concept I am talking about in this chapter. Make-up sex is more about healing the wounds created by conflict and mov-ing on. However, the conflict created via verbal fencing and debate is itself an aphrodisiac because the woman is perceived as being a formidable opponent.

Courtesans were very popular during a time in history when women in general were not allowed to read or write books, attend college, or debate men publicly. The courtesans were allowed to engage in all of these taboo behaviors because it made them more attractive sexual partners. Wives were not allowed to break the taboos because it kept them docile and easily controlled. Unfortunately, a docile and dumb partner is not that sexually exciting to most men. So the system required two separate types of women in order for the needs of men to be completely fulfilled.

Although women have made major advances over the last few hundred years, some remnants of the old ways of thinking always continue to color our thinking and our behavior until we educate ourselves otherwise. I certainly would have never guessed that men would find an uppity and feisty woman more attractive than a demure and placating female. Even in our modern times, the "nice" girls always seem to get the guys. The distinction I failed to make was that some men marry one kind of woman but prefer to have sex with another kind of woman. This is the Whore/Madonna Complex we hear so much about.

The Whore/Madonna Complex refers to the phenomenon in which some men view a woman as either a whore or a madonna. The whore is sexually available and desirable, but the madonna is seen as asexual and pure. A man operating from this worldview will usually lose sexual interest in his wife because she is his wife and because she is the mother of his children. He cannot relate to her as a fully functioning sexual being as long as she is in the role of wife and/or mother.

Most men have resolved their extreme feelings along these lines and can accept a female partner that is at once "naughty" and "nice." But some poor souls still cling to the idea that the mother of their children has to be held in such high regard that touching her sexually becomes taboo. Of course, the very idea that sexual touching is less than high regard for her is faulty. As is the idea that mothers don't have sex. Sex is how a woman becomes a mother, as we all know. But some people do act as if they have forgotten this simple biological fact when they act like sex is offensive or contraindicated to motherhood. Of course it should go without saying that mothers need and deserve sex just as much as other people.

If you believe that your man has a problem relating to you as a sexual being because you are his wife and/or the mother of his children, you may want to suggest he see a therapist. Some therapists believe the Whore/Madonna Complex arises from unresolved childhood issues with the man's mother.

As a woman, I also bought into the Whore/Madonna Complex to some degree. I was afraid of seeming too sexual, so I would hide my true sexual feelings and pretend to be pure. It was a façade that did not last long, obviously. I couldn't handle being less than authentic, and the truth is that I love sex and always have.

If you want to be sexually exciting, you will most likely need to abandon the idea of being pure and feigning indifference to sexual matters. Some men find women who seem innocent and inexperienced to be a turn-on, but most men are drawn to the wild woman. That attraction has been proven time and again by escorts and courtesans through the ages. The best part is that by allowing yourself the freedom to be sexually aware and aroused, you will enjoy sex more.

Great sex requires more than wild abandon. Truly great sex engages the intellect as well. If you explore the brainy side of sex, you will tap into a level of eroticism that has been highly prized through the ages. Intellectual stimulation has limitless potential and can be accessed regardless of physical limitations such as age or health. It may also be the most liberating experience of your life.

Intellectual stimulation can be broken down into verbal fencing, humor, active listening, sexual innuendo, and sharing secrets.

I have already made it clear that most men are aroused by a woman who is intelligent and assertive. Verbal fencing uses these attributes by approaching conversation as an opportunity to "show your stuff." Rather than adhering to the stereotypical female pattern of agreeing with the man and deferring to his "wisdom and experience," a courtesan will challenge his beliefs and conclusions. Verbal fencing is very much like actual fencing. If you are not careful, both parties can get hurt, so it is important to bring your metaphorical blade close to your partner without actually cutting him. If he is game, what ensues is a series of "thrusts and parries" with words.

It is also important to balance your desire to win with a sense of humor—not unlike that required for any other game or sport. Humor not only keeps conflict from becoming too adversarial, but adds its own erotic element to our interactions. When we laugh, we release many endorphins that are the same chemicals present when we have orgasms. Endorphins create a sense of well-being. Endorphins also bond us to others, so laughter can be a wonderful precursor to sex!

This may come as a surprise, but learning to listen to your partner is one of the best ways to boost your sex appeal and improve your sex life. My active listening skills were invaluable as an escort. In case you haven't already noticed, men love to talk about themselves, and most find a receptive and attentive listener extremely gratifying. In all fairness, both men and women love to be truly listened to. When we perceive that the listener has really understood and appreciated what we are sharing with them, we feel accepted and valuable as human beings. Simply nodding your head and saying "uh huh" does not communicate the level of engagement required for active listening. It is important to comment on a few of the details shared with you and to show some enthusiasm for the subject matter.

If you find the topic boring, remember that you care about this person. Surely you can at least be enthusiastic about your enjoyment of his level of excitement, regardless of the topic.

For instance, you might say "I just love to see you so happy," instead of attempting to feign interest in the topic that is causing him to be happy. That way you are expressing authentic emotion, which is vitally important if you want to keep the passion alive in your relationship.

Along with using verbal fencing, humor, and active listening techniques, employing the subtle use of sexual innuendo can make for stimulating conversation. Sexual innuendo takes a little practice to carry off successfully; timing is of the utmost importance. Similar to humor, sexual innuendo said in one context can be erotic while in another context can seem silly. Obviously, you don't want to have your attempt at being sexually suggestive turn out embarrassing, but how do you avoid it?

First, you need to know your audience—in this case, your husband or boyfriend. If you are uncertain whether he will appreciate a sexually suggestive reference, joke, story, or flirtation, you might want to hold off until you are sure. Everyone has different tastes, and what offends one will titillate another. My husband and I have both had occasional difficulties anticipating whether something we found humorous or sexually titillating would have the same effect on the other. With someone I don't know all that well, I usually refrain from sexually suggestive remarks or stories until I get to know them better. This is not about the level of physical intimacy you have shared, but how much you really know about their core values.

It is the core values we hold that tend to shape our sense of humor and eroticism. And unlike most other humor, sexual humor can turn out disastrously. Not only do you risk not eliciting a laugh, but you run the risk of offending your listener deeply. It is very easy to violate sexual taboos and, of course, that would have the opposite of the desired effect. Instead of turning him on, you leave an awful taste in his mouth.

With so much at risk, why even bother? Well, I have found that men are particularly enamored with sexual innuendo from a woman to whom they are attracted. It is as if you are one of the boys, part of the club, in the secret society of men … you pick a euphemism but hopefully you get the point. It can be rather delicious if done well by a female from whom one might otherwise not expect it. Sexual innuendo pairs with feigned sexual innocence and/or reluctance very well. It can be a way of catching him off guard and delighting him with an unexpected dose of sexual frankness.

I routinely employed the contrast between the good girl and the bad girl as a technique for arousing sexual desire. My clients particularly enjoyed it when I behaved with an almost overly stated professional demeanor and suddenly surprised them with a raw reference to anatomy or a specific sex act. It seems nothing is quite as enticing as a seemingly unavailable woman unexpectedly expressing her carnality.

Finally, part of stimulating the brain in a sexual manner involves the sharing of secrets. Long thought the province of females, secrets are in fact a prized part of male life as well. Men carry some secrets longer than women tend to, and they may confide in fewer individuals than most women do. But that only makes the secret that much more potent for him. Of course, the best way to get another person to share his secrets with you is to share your secrets with him. Too many women make the mistake of asking their man whether he has any secrets, which feels more like a form of entrapment. No one wants to feel like he is being interrogated. And everyone needs to be reassured that their secrets will be treated with respect and accorded privacy.

So if you want the sharing of secrets to enhance your shared sex life, you have to abide by a few rules. Never laugh at a secret. Never tell someone else's secret to another person. Never use a secret shared in a tender moment as a weapon during an argument. Remember, you are building trust that will not only enhance your sex life but your relationship in general. Treat that trust as something sacred, and you will be rewarded with more trust.

In the final analysis, the things that go to make up intellectual stimulation are components of healthy intimacy in any romantic relationship. It might seem strange that an escort would have something to share about emotional intimacy, but in fact, high-end escorting is all about emotional intimacy. I hope your improved intimacy bears you many fruits!

11

Taking Time to Date, Again

For those of you in a long-term relationship, you may think dating is behind you. Not so fast. Dating is an erotic art that should be a part of your love life as long as you are alive. Making a date with your partner regardless of how long you have known each other builds excitement, anticipation, and communicates how special your relationship is.

Even if you have known your partner for years, there is something special about dressing up and going out that simply cannot compare to all the foreplay in the world. Perhaps it is the anticipation of things to come that builds your excitement and helps to stoke passion's fires. Or maybe it is being removed from the surroundings of your everyday life and thrust into an environment that is at once unfamiliar as well as unpredictable. Certainly, seeing your partner in attire that says you are worth the effort doesn't hurt either. And when you dress up, you can't help but feel sexy and alive!

Although you may be tempted to go straight to a private romantic interlude, it is very important that you set aside several days or evenings each month to go out with your special someone. The rituals that surround dating are just as important—perhaps even more important—in established relationships than they are when we are getting acquainted. Getting out of the house and away from your daily obligations will renew your passions for each other and life in general.

Although it may be comfortable to spend time with your mate in front of the television watching a rented movie or at the local dog park walking the family dog, these activities take the edge off eroticism precisely because they are comfortable. To be sure, you want this level of friendship in your relationship, but to keep the sexual spark alive, you will need to get out of your comfort zone from time to time.

Keeping your sex life fresh and vibrant is really about remaining open to new experiences and new sensations. Rather than focus on what you do in the privacy of your bedroom, I recommend putting more planning and effort into dating your partner. This, after all, is where the first romantic moments in your life no doubt began! Because we are all individuals, there really is no such thing as a "perfect" date for everyone. However, if you take a chance and try a few different activities and venues, you might discover some new favorites.

A memorable date usually involves a long luxurious dinner at a fine restaurant where all your senses are engaged. Your sense of sight is titillated by the expert arrangement of the food, the table, and the restaurant décor. The sight of your date is also an aphrodisiac as he has undoubtedly dressed for the occasion. Your sense of smell is aroused by the aroma of the food and perhaps a light whiff of cologne emanating from your dinner partner.

Food that has crossed over into the domain of cuisine is one of the most intoxicating experiences your taste buds will ever encounter. And if you appreciate fine wine or spirits, your sense of taste will be further engaged. Your sense of touch is also involved in the pursuit of culinary perfection. Some foods are juicy; others are dry and brittle; and still others are soft and warm. And last but not least, your sense of hearing comes into play in a pleasing way during a fine dining experience in the form of your lover's voice.

The conversation with your companion can wander where it will but try topics that are intellectually stimulating. You should void topics that are related to your household obligations, the children, or other family affairs. Instead, focus on things you both find interesting but a little unfamiliar, such as current affairs, sports, or even politics. In this way, you will both be able to appreciate your partner in a different light, which will have the natural effect of re-igniting your sexual interest in each other.

Depending on your destination when you leave the restaurant, your attire should be chosen accordingly. If you are going to a cultural event, a movie, music concert, or the local theatre, you might dress more informally. If you are going to the symphony, the opera, or a musical, you will want to dress a little more formally, perhaps even semi-formally. Try wearing an evening dress that is cut a little low in the neckline or bares your back. While you want to choose attire that reflects your own unique sense of style, be sure to give yourself permission to take some risks. Don't be afraid to add a few sexy accents to your look!

I might wear a classic black cocktail dress cut just a little too short, and my shoes are never ordinary. I have always found that men love sexy shoes. Even if my attire is otherwise conservative, I like to add a sexy twist with a pair of ankle-strap heels, open-toed heels, or strappy evening sandals. With the right pair of heels, even a pinstripe suit can become sexy. However, if you plan on doing much walking on your date, you will want to bring something elegant and sexy that allows you to walk comfortably. Moderate heels would no doubt be better than four-inch heels, for instance, so bring both! Nothing says you can't wear high heels to dinner and low heels for the moonlit walk.

In addition, consider wearing something sheer under your blazer or jacket to add a little mystique. Skirts with slits are equally alluring because they create mystery and keep your admirers guessing. And, of course, your jewelry should be simple and tasteful. Jewelry works best when it accentuates your best features without taking attention away from you!

Men are usually less aware of the latest styles and trends and find sexy to be attractive no matter what Paris is doing this year. Of course, you don't want to look too dated, so some fashion consciousness in moderation will assure you that your look is both appropriate and appealing. When in doubt, I like to stick to the classic designs that are always in style. Women such as Audrey Hepburn and Jackie Onassis can serve as fashion guides to the classic looks. The way they dressed never goes out of style in large part because they found clothing that fit their lifestyles, personalities, and shapes and did not let fashion dictate otherwise. If you spend a little time familiarizing yourself with the cuts and colors of clothing that fit you best and most importantly make you feel great, you can begin to develop your own sense of style. This will communicate confidence, and as you have already learned, confidence is the sexiest thing going!

Activities that can increase the romantic quotient on your date include taking moonlit walks, touring art museums, and attending other people's weddings. The romantic elements of a moonlit walk seem obvious. You are alone; it is dark; and the moon is mysteriously lighting up your path. Holding hands is a natural impulse under these circumstances and might lead to a passionate kiss!

I have toured many art galleries and museums as an escort. It is a nice way to spend the afternoon before a romantic dinner. Art museums may seem a bit of a long shot on the romance scale, but trust me, they are quite romantic with the right person. Art arouses your senses and awakens you to thoughts and feelings out of the ordinary realm of your day-to-day life. If you share these thoughts and feelings with another, you can both open up your senses and perceptions to new possibilities. It also gives you a chance to see each other in a different light. Sharing your likes and dislikes in art is another way to bond and increase your intimacy. Whenever you have the chance to see an unfamiliar side of your partner, you risk falling in love with him all over again.

If art museums are difficult to come by where you live, you might try local gardens or parks. I have spent more than one date wandering parklike settings of beautifully landscaped gardens open to the public. Connecting with nature is a natural prelude to romance. And the gardens arouse all our senses with the gorgeous colors of flowers and leaves, the intoxicating fragrances of blossoms and earth, the heavenly sound of song birds, and the pleasant feel of a manicured lawn. Somehow, a stolen kiss in these surroundings is just that much more intoxicating.

Any entertainment can be fun on a date, but some forms of entertainment arouse your senses in such a way that your thoughts naturally turn to romance. The symphony is a fine example of a romantic pastime. Although it may seem boring to some since you are simply sitting while listening to classical music, the music itself can evoke many emotions. Remember my music of choice for seduction is either classical or new age. Music that engages all of our feelings produces the most romantic results. Classical music is crafted specifically to launch us on an emotional roller coaster. Attending the symphony is an excuse to get out of the house and dress up if you get tickets for the weekend. I recommend you try it at least once and see what develops.

Of course, sometimes we are not near a symphony. Certainly, other music can be romantic, too. An environment that would be more conducive to the type of romantic prelude you are attempting to create might be a jazz festival, an outdoor concert, or a piano bar. The point is to seek environments that are not an ordinary part of your daily life. It is with that first break from your normal routine that you open the door to the magic of romance.

Another place to listen to music and perhaps dance with your lover is at other people's weddings. Weddings can be a great place to recharge the romance in a long-term relationship. Having experienced this firsthand with my own husband, it seems to be a wonderful opportunity to be reminded of all the reasons you got married in the first place and reconnect with the emotions of your own wedding day. If you aren't married, you may still find yourself reminiscing about sentimental moments from your shared past. What could be more romantic?

Obviously, if you are not in a long-term relationship, you are no doubt already aware that dating has a place in your life today. However, you now have information that can transform an ordinary date into a romantic interlude to remember. Have fun engineering your perfect date. Hopefully, it will become habit-forming. There certainly are worse ways to spend your spare time. Be sure to read on. Next we take the date into the bedroom!

12

Asserting Healthy Boundaries

You might think it strange to discuss healthy boundaries in a book about sex. However, I would have made a really lousy escort if I had not had healthy boundaries. I certainly would not have enjoyed my profession as much as I did. And before I learned how to assert healthy boundaries, I really could not enjoy sex to its fullest.

Women in particular have difficulty asserting healthy boundaries. We may know how to slam the door entirely, but can we stay and play without giving up our space? And once engaged in an interaction with a male in particular, we women are more likely to make excuses for giving up what is important to us in order to avoid conflict or avoid appearing selfish. It is particularly taboo for women to say "no" to pleasing others or "yes" to pursuing our own needs and pleasures.

You might think of boundaries as a field or park in which you are safe to let down your guard, play, and have fun. Unless you know where the park begins and ends, you don't know where it is safe to play, so you might be on edge anticipating the unknown. But knowing the limits or boundaries in which you are playing can actually allow you to relax and let go more than you could without them!

In addition, good communication skills are absolutely required for a good sex life because sex is itself a form of communication. You need good communication skills so you can let your partner know what you like and don't like, what feels good and what does not feel good. You also need to be able to communicate with skill if you want to improve the level of intimacy in your relationship. Healthy boundaries are actually an integral part of successful communication, deeper intimacy, and fantastic sex!

In the beginning of my career as an escort, I had not perfected my assertion skills, and I was unclear about what my boundaries were. Even if I knew what some of my boundaries were, I was afraid to communicate them for fear of appearing too rigid or uptight. Little did I know that if I had been clear about my boundaries, first with myself and then with others, I would actually have come across as more relaxed and fun loving! But I thought appearing open to others' input even when I knew I was not would go over better. I wanted to "go along to get along."

For instance, the use of a condom can be a bone of contention with clients. Some simply do not want to wear one and will offer excuses, explanations, and even more money in an attempt to talk an escort out of her health and safety. In the beginning, I would try to smile sweetly and use my sexiest voice to say I couldn't possibly have sex without a condom. My voice and my body language were apologizing all over the place. Apparently, I didn't think I had a right to say "no" firmly. I thought it was my duty to be nice. And I was certain men would respond more favorably to a feminine approach.

I was wrong. The nice and feminine approach only invited them to persist in their efforts to convince me to do something

I did not want to do. They thought they stood a chance of wearing down my defenses, so they only increased the intensity of their begging, pleading, or threatening. Finally I abandoned my nice girl approach and simply said "no" firmly and emphatically, and then I changed the topic. I didn't wait to see how they felt about my "no." I just assumed they had no choice but to accept it and moved on. That is an example of a healthy boundary. It is not nice or mean. It is not angry or afraid. It simply is without apology or approval. It just is.

Healthy boundaries enable us to say "no" to things we don't want to be available for, but they also let us say "yes" to the things we want. Healthy boundaries also establish safety for the people with whom we are in a relationship because they let them know what is okay and what is not okay when they are dealing with us. It also gives them permission to establish their own set of healthy boundaries with us.

One of the reasons I was a successful escort was because I learned to be very clear about my boundaries. I communicated what I was available for and what I was not available for. Men knew where they stood with me, and this created a level of comfort and security, even if at times it also created some disappointment. By establishing my boundaries at the beginning of a relationship, I also opened a dialog that allowed the other person to discuss his feelings and perceptions. He could let me know what he wanted and what he did not want. He could also let me know what he was confused or conflicted about.

Even when men are paying for sex, they can find it very difficult to ask for what they want. Often, they are too embarrassed or ashamed to communicate clearly. So I would model clear communication for them, and it would have the net result of making them feel better about being straightforward, too. It wasn't that most men had such unusual desires. But the fact that their desires were "normal" or "vanilla" did not make it any easier for them to express themselves.

For example, when I had made it clear that I always used a latex barrier and never provided anal intercourse, it paved the way for men to tell me what they were hoping for or to ask me questions about the kinds of sex I would do. It turns out that healthy boundaries can be a great icebreaker for conversations about sex!

After you know your own boundaries and wish to have those boundaries respected, you need to know how to communicate your boundaries to others. First of all, it can help to understand the difference between asserting yourself and being aggressive. Aggression can be defined as a forceful action or procedure, especially when intended to dominate or master. On the other hand, to assert yourself can be defined as to compel recognition, especially of one's rights. Simply put, when you are being assertive, you just say how things are *for you* and make no attempt to control or judge or intimidate the other person.

If your partner refuses to acknowledge your boundaries as stated, you must take the responsibility for removing yourself from that person and/or situation. He will learn rather quickly that you mean business, and will either choose to moderate his behavior or spend time without you. But, you need not state that explicitly as a threat … that would come off as aggressive.

After you start operating from a place of having healthy boundaries, you will also have to honor the boundaries of others. If someone tries to pass off an attempt at controlling you as if it is a boundary, you don't have to honor that. For example, if after you state your boundaries, your partner says he will no longer perform your favorite sex act, perhaps he is trying to be manipulative. But if he is simply stating what works or does not work for him, you must either choose to honor that boundary by moderating your behavior, or you must honor that boundary by removing yourself.

If you are experienced in negotiating and communicating clearly, you will be able to talk to your partner about your sexual needs, desires, dislikes, and wants with ease. You will also know how to listen to his needs, desires, dislikes, and wants. And neither of you will assume that you must give the other everything they want just because they want it. You can negotiate for what you both want and find compromises that keep both of you extremely happy.

For instance, let's say your man wants you to perform a sex act that you find disgusting. You might initially feel obligated to fulfill his request to keep the peace or hang on to the relationship. This is a terrible idea. By agreeing to do something you hate, you are sentencing yourself to repeat performances. You are also communicating that sex is more for him than you. A more positive approach is to honestly tell him you have no interest in this sexual activity, but you are interested in something else—provided you are interested in a particular sex act. For many men, the simple fact that you demonstrate interest and enthusiasm for sex of any kind will be a turn-on.

I used this method of problem solving with my clients all the time. Rather than say no and stop there, I preferred to say no, but how about this alternative? I was negotiating while staying true to my own values and preferences. It proved to be a very successful way to maintain my boundaries while fulfilling men's sexual fantasies. I learned that most men suggest sexual positions and techniques because they may be feeling bored or uninspired, and they want to add excitement. Basically, I met that desire for excitement and/or variety by redirecting them to sexual activities that I found pleasing. There is no reason this can't work equally well for you. Just remember that negotiation and compromise work best when used in concert with healthy boundaries—especially when it comes to sex!

13

Taking the Lead in the Bedroom

I have already discussed the very popular sexual fantasy among men of being seduced by a woman. I went into detail about how and why men crave a sexually assertive female, but I didn't tell you how to seduce a man. In this chapter I will give you all the information you need to become an experienced and skilled seductress.

You may already consider yourself quite adept at attracting and seducing men. But I would bet that your technique falls short of initiating sex. Most women learn ways of making themselves desirable so that overwhelming sexual desire will compel the man to make the first move. As women we may know how to frame our physiques with the proper clothing such as thongs, push-up bras, bikinis, short skirts, long dresses split up the side, snug sweaters, or our favorite pair of high heels. Most women learn to accentuate their face with the right eye shadow, mascara, lip gloss, or rouge. And we women adorn our ear lobes, necks, hands, feet, belly buttons, and ankles with anything from costume jewelry to gold chains to pearls to diamonds.

Many of us learn mannerisms and ploys to attract the man of our desires. We may employ a bashful or innocent look by batting our eyes and parting our lips just so. Our message might be one of inexperience waiting to be taught. Perhaps you ignore the man who has caught your eye and make him work extra hard to get your attention. In this case, your message might be one of experience waiting to be impressed. There are, of course, many points in between these two extremes. I have personally used both extremes to attract men, and they both work very well. And I have approached courtship from the more down-to-earth perspective of just being myself. I have to admit that being straightforward may be an excellent way to secure a life partner, but it seems to lack some of the juice—the sexual excitement and tension—of courtship rituals.

Whatever style you gravitate toward when you are intentionally attempting to attract the attentions of the opposite sex, you will need to put them aside if you are to learn how to initiate sex with a man. It's nice to know how to be both the passive partner waiting to be swept off her sexual feet and the assertive partner who can do the sweeping. There are some sexual scenarios that are mutual in every respect where neither person seduces or is seduced, but these are rather rare in my experience. It is more likely that one partner will tend to initiate sex before the other does, and this has a tendency to frame the encounter.

When I was new to escorting, I would wait for the man to make the first move. The only thing I knew about seducing a man was how to attract his attention and encourage him. I might ignore some of his passes without getting offended or offering encouragement. This usually had the effect of reassuring him that it was okay to proceed with a gradual and cautious seduction. I guess I liked to use a combination of playing hard to get and making myself available. It worked. But it was one-sided. I was lost the first time a man asked me to seduce him. I thought I had been seducing men with my feminine wiles all along. So what more could I do?

What I didn't realize was that most women's definitions of seduction are only about attracting the sexual attentions of a man. There is a huge difference between attracting your object of affection and actually reaching out and taking what you want. So for the purposes of this chapter, I will be using the terms "seduction" and "initiating sex" interchangeably. Really, I am going to show you some of the seduction techniques that men use on women. Turns out many men are just waiting for us women to turn the tables on them!

When my clients asked me to make love to them and/or seduce them, I enjoyed beginning with comments about their appearance. Telling a man how attractive and sexy he is may not come naturally to us as women because we are used to procuring compliments rather than dispensing them. But it can actually be quite a turn-on for both you and your man.

Giving compliments arouses me as well as the person I am complimenting. Words are powerful, and they can create a lot of sexual heat without lifting a finger. I never make stuff up or lie. I can find something to admire about anyone, and I focus on that. It may be the color of his eyes, the shape of his posterior, the bulge in his biceps, the sound of his voice, the smell of his hair, the size of his penis, the way he walks, or even something more intangible and abstract such as his intelligence. Whatever it is that makes this man sexy, I accentuate it by giving it my unbridled admiration.

After you have convinced him that you cannot resist him, rather than simply acquiesce to his advances as may be your habit, you want to beat him to the punch and make the first move. The first move for some women means either taking off their own clothes or unzipping his pants to give him a blow job. This is not the type of seduction I am trying to share with you. Instead, you want to keep the focus off of yourself and put it all on him. And you don't want to rush to a sexual act. You want to take your time with lots of foreplay. Begin the same way you would love to be seduced. If you are like me, you want to be complimented and then you want to be kissed. Initiating a kiss rather than accepting a kiss is actually quite different, so you may need to practice a few times.

I have found that I have better success when initiating a kiss if I have built up the tension to that moment. Verbal foreplay with compliments and sexual innuendo is very helpful in accruing sexual tension, as is some carefully placed touching. During the course of the evening, you can begin building toward that kiss by discretely touching his hands, arms, shoulders, back, and face. You want to avoid touching anything that might make your sexual intentions completely clear. The point is to create sexual tension, and the way to do that is to create familiarity tinged with a slight suggestion of sex. Subtle sexual cues are much more erotic because they keep us a little confused, and we have to wait. That combination can build our sexual excitement to the point where we are about to explode!

Have you ever been kissed by a man who had just one kiss that he obviously gave every woman he ever dated? I have, and it always makes me feel like I'm not even there. Men who kiss this way don't adjust their kisses to the subtle cues of their lovers. You certainly don't want to make that mistake. You have to adjust your kiss to your partner's preferences and mood. You may be ready to give him a French kiss, but he may tighten his jaw to prevent your tongue from entering. It won't be a hostile maneuver, just a barely noticeable grimace on his part. So if you pay attention as if kissing were dancing, you can move with your partner while still taking the lead.

Taking the lead means you don't rush in until you have his cooperation, but you don't give up either. So wait a few beats and try to make the kiss more intimate again. In this way, you are being persistent with your desire but not offensive. Most importantly, you are giving his sexual desire a chance to catch up with yours. Seduction requires some finesse and patience. You have to be willing to take a little mild rejection, adjust your advances accordingly, and then continue to seduce.

Kissing becomes permission to try the next step in foreplay. Again and again you will be engaging in this dance of subtle cues. When you take things a step further, you want to remain aware of your lover's mood. He may relax, or he may stiffen. If he is rigid anywhere but his penis, you are moving too fast. Fortunately a man's penis will give you many clues to his state of mind and level of sexual arousal, so as a woman you will have a distinct advantage during foreplay. But don't let his penis be the ultimate authority about his desire. Some men don't agree with their penises, and you must honor that. If he says he isn't in the mood, take him at his word regardless of whether he has an erection or not.

If he is in the mood, then move ahead with more foreplay. Savor each part of his body beginning with his neck and ear lobes and moving down to his nipples and belly. Unbutton his shirt seductively but keep his pants on for a while so that neither of you puts all the focus on his penis. He may not think his upper body provides him with much sexual pleasure, but you can show him otherwise. I have educated many men about their erogenous zones, and they have been very grateful. Remember to take the lead here and tell him to be patient if he tries to take over and tell you what to do. I sometimes tell the impatient man a little joke such as "good things come to boys who wait" and then continue my slow seduction.

You want to try to strike a balance between making him wait and keeping things hot. Remember, a man's sexual response heats up more quickly than most women's, so you don't need to ply him with hours of foreplay even if that is something you require from him. Your focus is on him at this point, and you will find that initiating sex creates its own sexual heat for you. You may not even need foreplay when you are the sexual aggressor. It can be a powerful aphrodisiac all by itself. I find that I become aroused in a completely different way when I initiate sex. My clitoris becomes rock hard and I break out in a light sweat. I hope you have fun finding out what taking the sexual lead does to you!

Now try copping a feel of his genitals through his clothing before you ever take his pants off. Being touched through one's clothing can actually feel sexier than direct contact. It also feels very sexy to reach down into his pants and grab his penis (careful with your fingernails!).

At this point, if you haven't already done so, you want to get him on his back, and my favorite way of doing this is to push him down. I usually aim for his chest muscles and use the palm of one or both hands. Men are bigger than us in most cases, so it takes a little determination and strength on your part, but don't hit him. You can easily hurt a man if you assume you can't, so be careful. Your effort needs to exceed gentle but fall short of being forceful. Incorporate a mischievous smile as you push him onto his back so that he knows you don't mean him any harm. I have done this to hundreds of men, and they are usually quite turned on by it. The point is to overwhelm and overpower him with the strength of your sexual desire while reassuring him that he can trust you to take good care of him.

As the one initiating sex, your next move wouldn't be to just lay down next to him. Instead, you want to get on top of him. My favorite position is straddling the middle of his body so I have equal access to his face and his genitals. From this vantage point, you can continue seducing your man in a variety of ways. You might initiate sexual intercourse in the position known as the Isis Squat (see Chapter 23) or perhaps mutual oral sex in the position called a 69 (look at the number 6 and the number 9 for clues, or simply put your mouth on his penis and your vagina in his face—that's a 69!). If he is in a good mood and highly aroused, you might decide to sit on his face. But don't do this unless you are certain he likes it and is willing at this moment. When in doubt, your seductions should focus on providing him sexual pleasure so that he feels swept off his feet!

If you are anything like me, just reading about this might be getting you hot. But don't lose your cool. We still have much more to learn before we are ready to consummate this long seduction, so go to the next chapter quickly!

14

Using Ritual, Timing, and Ambience

Escorts approach sex as an extremely important event worthy of all the anticipation, planning, and effort most people expend for other special occasions such as birthdays, anniversaries, holidays, vacations, and so on.

Although I wasn't in love with my clients, I made every effort to honor sex as a special and sacred event. Everything I did went into creating potency in the sexual encounter simply because it was exalted in my mind as an extremely important part of life. So many people waste precious energy on shame, guilt, and embarrassment when that energy could be used to create sensuality, intimacy, and meaningful sexual moments.

Before I ever met a man, I took the time to find out something about his likes and dislikes over the telephone. I didn't approach this like I was taking his order for a meal. Instead, I was subtle and a little mysterious. I used my intuition to fill in the gaps between what he actually said and what he told me about himself. If he mentioned a lot of stress at work, I knew it would be best for me to create a relaxing and soothing atmosphere in anticipation of his arrival. But if he complained about being bored, I would ensure lots of excitement when he walked through my door.

For the bored client, I used what I liked to call my multimedia presentation. I wore bold-colored lingerie such as red or purple garters and stockings. I kept the lighting in the room bright by letting a little sunlight filter through the curtains and played upbeat classical tunes on my stereo. I put one of my personal adult films into the DVD player so he could watch me on television while he talked to me in person. Rather than put him to sleep with a massage, I would invite him to receive a blow job in front of my wall mirror so he could watch our sexual interaction in the mirror as well as in person. Needless to say, this created a level of exhilaration that met with the greatest of approval.

For the stressed client, I created a soothing, healing, and nurturing place for him to escape to with the subdued lighting of candles, the subtle aroma of incense, new age music, and the gentle trickle of several water fountains. I would greet him at the door with a sparkling water and let him sit and talk about the troubles of his day. But I wouldn't wait long to invite him to disrobe for a relaxing massage. While I massaged him with aromatherapy massage lotion, I encouraged him to breath deeply to help relax his tensions away. Sex flowed slowly and easily from this place of tranquility.

As we move into the section of this book that discusses sexual technique, it is important to keep some intangibles in mind if you want to ensure that your sexual technique flows naturally and beautifully from your core. Ritual, timing, ambiance, and intention are instrumental in adding an erotic and spiritual dimension to sex and ensuring that your sexual technique is never mechanical or routine.

In addition to empowering yourself as a fully sexual being, acknowledging the very human need for ritual will add an unexpected dimension to your sex life. Humans have shown an affinity for ritual since the dawn of history. Ritual is simply defined as "any customary observance or practice." As such, you are free to establish your own rituals. After these rituals become part of your interaction with your partner, they take on a life of their own. Rituals have the power to evoke strong emotions because they remind us of past events and encounters.

Ritual can incorporate tangible objects. You might set aside a special pillow or rug that is just for lovemaking. You can have lingerie for everyday sex and lingerie set aside for very special sexual events. A favorite musical composition or album can signal to your senses that sex is in the air. Saving a particular fragrance or scented oils just for your romantic interludes can be particularly powerful because our memories are so intricately tied to our sense of smell.

As you construct your own sexual ritual, also pay attention to the order in which you do things. Perhaps you enjoy a shower followed with the application of your favorite body lotion by your lover. Or you might prefer light conversation accompanied by your favorite beverage while wearing a seductive slip. These sexual cues become shorthand for future interludes. The ability for these rituals to arouse us in the future amplifies their erotic potential through repetition and timing.

Timing comes into play not only when we set a date for sex, but also in the way we approach seduction. Timing is the key ingredient in both humor and sex. Have you ever heard someone tell a perfectly good joke with the wrong timing? The joke falls flat, and no one laughs. The same words are being said, but the timing is what makes or breaks the joke. Without timing, words are not funny no matter how many times you repeat them. The same applies to sex. Sexy is as sexy does, and timing is what makes something we do sexy. The way the actresses in the black-and-white movies of old crossed their legs, lit their cigarettes, walked across a room, or batted their eyes was terribly sexy. But if their timing had been different, these same physical actions would have been transformed from sexy to slapstick.

Obviously, the key to good timing is to be neither too late nor too early. You want to be on the mark time-wise. But how do you know when and for how long to do anything to create sex appeal? One way I perfected my timing was by watching those old movies I mentioned. Most modern entertainment has lost touch with something as subtle as timing. Movie producers are aiming for fast action and shocking visual images so that viewers are more overwhelmed than entertained. But movies from the '30s, '40s, and '50s used timing to titillate. You might consider spending a few afternoons studying women like Lauren Bacall, Katherine Hepburn, and Ingrid Bergman.

Lauren Bacall is particularly magnetic in 1940s movies such as *To Have and Have Not*, *Key Largo*, and *Dark Passage*. You can listen to her verbal delivery and look at movie stills on this excellent and entertaining website: http://themave.com/Bacall/BBv3. The sexual energy between Lauren Bacall and Humphrey Bogart is a lesson in the art of seduction all its own. They not only generated sparks on camera, they were lovers and eventually became husband and wife in real life. Bacall's timing in front of the camera and her verbal delivery are impeccable.

Katherine Hepburn is a particularly intriguing study in timing as she knitted sex appeal and humor together in a seamless and enchanting fashion. Her movie career is an illustrious one, and I highly recommend you see her in *The Philadelphia Story* (1940), which also stars Jimmy Stewart and Cary Grant. *Bringing Up Baby* (1938) is my personal favorite, because I find the sexual tension and humor are expertly balanced to play the viewer's emotions like a fine musical instrument. Hepburn reminds us that we need not take sex so seriously and we can have a great deal of fun with it!

Ingrid Bergman may just be one of the most intoxicating women to ever grace the silver screen. She is, of course, most famous for her role starring opposite Humphrey Bogart in *Casablanca*. But you will also find many memorable performances in a variety of films spanning her career, which lasted 50 years. Alfred Hitchcock's *Notorious* (1946) allowed Bergman a great deal of emotional complexity, which contains many elements of excellent timing. With her expert sense of timing, Bergman succeeds in blending wholesomeness with smoldering sexuality. Timing in this case is more a matter of patiently allowing one's eyes to say it all.

It is not easy to teach proper timing. Some would say you either have it or you don't. But I believe you can learn to improve your timing. In large part, timing is a function of intuition. If you relax into the moment and trust your gut feelings to guide you, you will achieve better results in all facets of your life, but especially when it comes to sex. Where so many people have difficulty is in simply doing nothing. Timing requires a moment of waiting—a slight pause. Take a deep breath, stop thinking, and allow your feelings to wash over you. When you are relaxed and in touch with your own feelings, it is much easier to ascertain what your partner is feeling and to interpret the moment. You will feel the energy between you, and this will guide your next move.

The single most important thing you can do to perfect your timing and create sexual sparks is to practice that slight pause. Take your focus off outside stimuli and turn inward; breathe slowly and deeply to clear your mind of thoughts. This will help you get centered and become in tune with your own desire. You want your sexuality to spring from deep inside of you, and that requires a moment of quiet. You can do this throughout any of life's activities, but should especially at any stage of a sexual encounter with your partner. It's not necessary for this meditative moment to be obvious to anyone else, as it can take as little as 30 seconds.

During that time you are tapping into your own sexual desire and unique rhythms. You are also allowing your partner's anticipation to build. The number one rule about timing is to slow down. Rushing through sex is like wolfing down a gourmet meal. You don't get a chance to enjoy it. Sex is one time in your busy schedule when you must take your time if you want it to be truly fulfilling.

While you are setting the mood for your seduction, be clear on the ambiance or atmosphere you want to create. You need not adhere to the same ambiance every time you make love. Sometimes you may be in a playful mood, and other times you may be in the grips of a deep and burning love. Learning to go with these changing moods is part of learning to be spontaneous. So although you want to establish some ritual and expend some energy on preparing and planning ahead, you must strike a balance between that and just going with the flow. Don't be so rigid that you can't intuit the moment and act accordingly.

For instance, you may have gone to great lengths to create an exceedingly romantic and meaningful encounter, but when your lover shows up, he is in the mood for being irreverent and playful. Obviously there is some discrepancy between the ambiance for each of your moods. Both are fun, and both can be sexy. But they are very different. So what should you do? Of course, getting angry or trying to control your partner does nothing for either of your libidos. What you need to do is find a compromise between your two moods.

Sex does not have to be one extreme or another. And if you communicate your intentions prior to your rendezvous, your partner can be prepared for the frame of mind you are trying to create. For example, tell your partner that you want to be playful or meaningful (or someplace in between) *before* you get naked. After you are naked and sexually engaged, your feelings are likely to be much more vulnerable and potentially volatile. It is best to agree on an agenda—your preferred ambiance—before that happens.

Whether you are going for an ambiance that is light and frivolous or heavy with deep abiding love, you can create your chosen ambiance with a combination of the right lighting, music, scent, sights, ritual, and timing. If you want to communicate intense feelings of affection, you might pick earthy fragrances, classical music, red roses, silk sheets, and black lingerie. Your timing would slow down to reflect a certain air of reverence. Everything you do will communicate that this moment is very important.

A playful ambiance, on the other hand, might incorporate floral incense, popular tunes by your favorite vocalist, wild flowers, cotton sheets, and white lace lingerie. I would use ritual and timing to bring humor into play while I light the incense and begin my seduction. Telling jokes is perfectly appropriate if you want your sex to be light and playful. I have used humor on many occasions to infuse the sexual atmosphere with more spontaneity and a childlike vulnerability. Laughter is a great way to relax inhibitions and forget the day's cares. It gets us back into our bodies where great sex takes place!

Whereas ambiance is the mood you want to create, your intention is the anticipated outcome that guides your planned actions. Ultimately, your intention is to create wonderful sex. But why? Are you interested in reaching new orgasmic highs? Do you want to feel closer to your partner? Is there a sense of freedom and abandon that you are attempting to create in your life? Have you resolved to become the world's greatest lover? Are you hoping to fix other problems in your life through sex? Are you aware that sex can be a bridge to an improved spiritual life?

Knowing what your ultimate intentions are—the reasons behind the initial goal of great sex—will go a long way toward helping you avoid frustration and disappointment. Sex cannot fix the other problems in your life and shouldn't be used as a means to avoid larger issues that need your attention. Orgasms are a beautiful thing with powerful healing properties. Pursuing orgasms is a worthy goal simply for the sake of physical and mental health. Sex has the power to increase intimacy, but only if used in concert with healthy communication and problem solving.

If you are simply feeling trapped, bored, or in a rut, sex can be a wonderful catalyst for other changes in your world. I have seen many people initiate a long list of positive changes in their lives simply by breaking free sexually. Few women give much thought to becoming great lovers, so if you are one of the few who wish to add this to your list of accomplishments, I applaud you. The world needs more women like you! Sex and spirituality have a long mutual history, and you can realize many spiritual truths through certain sexual practices, which I will discuss later in this book.

Ultimately, you will decide which path works best for you as you pick and choose those things that resonate with your inner truth. Sex is an integral part of life, and the only reason there is life. I hope the subsequent chapters on technique will add immeasurably to your capacity to enjoy your sexuality. Above all else, remember to have fun experimenting!

15

Enjoying Porn

Escorts know men love porn so we use it in our profession. We may post naked photos of ourselves on our websites or even go so far as producing and starring in our own videos. Some clients like to take photos of escorts in various stages of undress, and those of us who agree to let them, usually charge extra for it. A few escorts will even make an adult video with the client in the starring role, charging him even more for that privilege.

Many women have negative views of sexually explicit material whereas men, regardless of what they claim to believe about porn, tend to enjoy it.

You may have very strong feelings about pornography. If you have ever viewed pornographic images, whether in the pages of a men's magazine or in an adult video, you may have felt angry or uncomfortable. Most pornography still follows rather predictable formulas that seem to adhere to male dominance and sexual coercion. Rather than present raw uncensored sexuality as a mutually pleasurable experience, some films seem to focus on ways in which males can either garner a laugh or two at the expense of women or derive a feeling of power over women.

Even in the most vanilla male-produced porn, the point of reference is decidedly male. For instance, when was the last time you had an actual orgasm because a warm sticky substance was squirted on your back, your chest, or your face? Unless you have an incredible imagination, I would bet the answer is never. Yet the bulk of mainstream porn depicts woman after woman experiencing mind-blowing orgasms while some guy ejaculates onto her. In reality, few men find this to be an activity that leads to their own orgasms, either.

Most men will keep their penis right where it is at the moment of ejaculation in order to maximize the moment of pleasure, unless of course, they watch a lot of porn. Then they may pull out at the last minute so they can see themselves ejaculate. A few women may find this erotic as well. That's fine. I have found it to be erotic at times, too. But erotic is a far cry from orgasmic. And, unfortunately, pornography that communicates something other than the truth about female sexual response tends to accomplish two things: first, it teaches men how to be terrible lovers; second, it insults women viewers by ignoring our very real sexual needs. Either way, the end result is less sexual satisfaction for the viewers of porn.

I would encourage you to embrace any frustration or anger you have about pornographic magazines and movies while keeping an open mind. You most likely haven't viewed all the pornographic images that exist, so it is possible that someone has photographed or filmed something that may actually work for both your genitals and your emotions. I certainly have discovered porn that works for me, and I am confident that you can find porn you can enjoy if you are willing to give it a try.

I recommend you select pornography that you feel good about in your mind as well as in your pants. Because both men and women are visual creatures, contrary to popular gender stereotypes, you owe it to yourself to maximize your potential for sexual enjoyment. Of course, the fact that your man might be forever grateful is a no-brainer.

Many bright and inventive producers are changing the pornographic landscape. You can find a variety of pornographic videos produced by women as well as married couples (I have listed some for you in the resource appendix of this book). These videos tend to feature actresses that have more natural and healthy bodies than those we usually associate with porn.

Not unexpectedly, the approach to sex is also more natural and healthy on many levels. The women tend to be more sexually empowered, and the sexual scenarios are usually consensual. Thankfully, an abundance of variety also exists, whether your fantasies are filled with romance and plenty of plot or lots of nudity and taboo.

You might begin your quest for proper porn by purchasing an instructional video. Although these videos show real live sex acts, they tend to do it with an academic flair. Consequently, x-rated footage is interspersed with instructional commentary from a doctor or sex therapist. My husband and I actually appeared in one of these videos. It was fun to make, and although the sex scenes are interrupted by a suited female in a classroom setting, the eroticism is still there. However, this approach is an admittedly mild introduction to porn and intended to be so.

If you would like a little porn while you learn, try any of the instructional videos produced by the Sinclair Institute. You can shop online at www.bettersex.com/default.asp where you will find everything from oral sex techniques to advanced sexual positions presented in an informative and erotic manner. These videos not only bring visual images of sex into your home, but they offer an opportunity for you and your man to discuss lovemaking techniques.

If you tend to prefer plot and romance, check out several videos produced by former film star Candida Royalle. She has built a solid reputation as a producer of female-centric porn. You will find titles that remind you more of the "bodice ripper" romance novels written for women than pornographic videos: *Rites of Passion, Revelations, Femme, Sensual Escape, A Taste of Ambrosia, The Gift, The Bridal Shower,* and more!

Another benefit to viewing videos produced with women in mind is that the male actors tend to be more attractive than those in mainstream heterosexual porn. I can only assume that some of the men who produce porn are either intimidated by attractive men, or they think their predominately male customers will be. How else can one explain the discrepancy? Whatever the reason, if you are not into fat, hairy, old men having sex with young girls with gigantic fake breasts, you will find most woman-produced porn a welcome change!

You might also want to treat yourself to videos produced by Andrew Blake. Begin by visiting his personal website to see whether you enjoy his photography at www.andrewblake.com. His videos are very much about beautiful images of beautiful women (most of them have natural breasts), and in many ways, he has developed his own form of erotic art. The mood he creates is very expensive, classy, and luxurious, and even the background music reflects this. My one criticism would be that he does not use enough men in his videos—but at least the men that he films are gorgeous!

In my work with men over the years, I have found sexually explicit images in the form of photos and videos to be very helpful. Most men respond very favorably to visual stimuli, and while I am putting all kinds of energy into making sure I am that visual stimuli, I also enjoy increasing the sexual tension with other visual stimulation. Some women may find the thought of this intimidating because it provides an opportunity to feel jealous of the women in the photos and/or videos. But if you remember that your man is in the room to have sex with you, then other images really hold no power over you, except to accentuate the erotic tone you are setting.

Of course, because I am fully aware that I am aroused by sexually explicit material, I am more focused on my own arousal than any feelings of jealousy or inferiority. Still, it can be an issue for either the man or the woman. Some men may worry that their genitals are not the same size as that of porn actors, and they may also worry that they can't stay as hard for as long as these actors seem to. Being a small-busted woman, I can feel intimidated by women with big breasts. You might find similar feelings come up for you regarding some other body part. The point is that no matter who we are or what we look like, we all have moments when we feel a little less than completely confident about ourselves.

Popular media images and advertising certainly don't help us feel good about ourselves. Why would they? There is no money in that. As consumers, we are more valuable to the companies that want to sell us products if we feel insecure, inferior, and incomplete. The more miserable we are, the more money we will hopefully spend in pursuit of whatever is being touted as a magic cure for what ails us. Our sexuality is attacked from every angle. We are told that our hips are too big, our breasts are too small, our breath stinks, our genitals stink, we have too much body hair, we have too little hair on our heads, our erections don't last long enough, and we are just too old for words. It's a wonder any of us still has the courage to have sex at all.

I encourage you to see these dollar-driven messages for the hostile brainwashing that they are. You are enough just the way you are. And fortunately, beauty begins inside of us, not on the outside. As for the outside—it seems we have all been told there is one way to be beautiful. Despite the fact that nature makes it abundantly clear that beauty and sexual attractiveness come in myriad forms, we humans think only certain hair color, height, and secondary sex characteristics are sexy. Some people are so submissive to these artificial beauty standards that when they do find themselves feeling sexually attracted to someone who does not conform to the standard, they become confused, disoriented, and even frustrated.

Well, it's really okay to have your own opinions about beauty. There is not one way or a right way to be beautiful. The erotic images that have been applauded as the ideal throughout the millennia have had little in common. Every hundred years, humans change their minds about what makes a woman beautiful to such a degree that a woman who was considered beautiful at one time would now be thought ugly. Whether you happen to conform to current beauty standards or not is really just an accident of birth. Had you been born during another time, you would be perceived differently.

I am able to appreciate a variety of body types, ages, races, and genders as beautiful. I feel good about myself, so it is easier to be generous with others. When I was working as an escort, I learned that men who felt confident and successful were much more positive, complimentary, and optimistic during our time together. It was the man who thought very little of himself who would dole out criticism and cynicism. If you find your man is less than supportive and complimentary to you—or makes the mistake of comparing you to images in magazines or film—you can rest assured that he is simply showing you signs of his own low self-esteem. Rather than give power to his words and waste one precious minute of your life worrying about yourself, you can put him on notice that you will not accept any such talk from him—ever.

After you have decided to use pornography in your sex life and have gone to the trouble to select a magazine or video that you think you will enjoy, how do you incorporate that into your lovemaking? You can just leave the magazine lying out for him to stumble across. Try the coffee table if you have no children or houseguests. The nightstand near your bed is another good location. You will thoroughly enjoy the look of surprise and delight that comes over the face of the man who has just discovered porn that his wife or girlfriend bought. Most men are so overwrought with joy they are speechless. For many men, it is as if you have entered their private world and become their best buddy.

You can also use the element of surprise with an adult video. You might sit down for a typical evening of television viewing and discretely hit the Play button on the VCR or DVD player. Very few porn films are ever viewed from beginning to ending. That would simply defeat the purpose of an adult movie. So if your man is like most men, he will probably forget all about his difficult day at work and the evening news and turn his attention to you!

When a man is thumbing through a pornographic magazine or watching an adult video, I sometimes enjoy engaging him in conversation about something else. I find that pairing visual stimulation with intellectual stimulation can be a very powerful combination. So while he is looking at full-color images of women's genitals, I might talk about the stock market or world affairs. There is something terribly exciting about doing something taboo while you act as if it is business as usual.

During sex, I like to have an x-rated video playing in the background. Rather than sit and watch it, I enjoy including it as part of a multi-media experience. So along with the candles, incense, sensual music, and lingerie, the adult video plays silently in the background offering peripheral or subconscious stimulation. I find it particularly sexy to glance over at the television screen to see someone else engaging in the very same sex act I am involved in at that moment. I might even make sure there is a large mirror on the wall right next to the television so I can look at both the porn actors and the reflection of my lover and me. If you are someone who enjoys watching, this is a supreme turn-on!

Be sure to experiment enough to decide what works best for you. Give yourself a chance to get past your initial embarrassment or perhaps feelings of disdain. It is only natural that you feel negative about sexually explicit images given the current sex-negative culture. But wouldn't you rather make up your own mind? The only way to do that is to actually view a variety of porn and see what you think of it—not what you are supposed to think about it—but what your true feelings are when no one is there to judge you or embarrass you.

For that reason, I suggest you screen the material you are thinking about incorporating into your sex life privately. If you don't find it offensive, then you can share it with your partner. Whatever you do, keep your focus on your pleasure and having fun. Who knows, while you are doing your pornographic research, you may find yourself overcome with passions of your own. There is no reason you can't try out the porn before you share it. Just lie back and let your fingers do the walking!

16

Utilizing Massage

Many of my clients came to me on edge, nervous, fearful, and exhausted. They thought sex would cure everything that ailed them. But too much stress can hamper sexual function, let alone sexual release. Although many of them worried that massage was just my attempt to avoid engaging in sex with them, they would nevertheless acquiesce to my demands that they get up on the massage table and let me do my thing. Soon, they were feeling so good they almost forgot they wanted to have sex. That level of forgetfulness or lack of self-consciousness was just what they needed to enjoy sex more fully.

Time and time again, I used a combination of deep massage and light stroking to lift the cares of the day and alleviate tired muscles, tension headaches, angry attitudes, and limp genitalia. Contrary to these men's first impulses, massage was the best route to the sex they craved. First, the body must be relaxed, and the mind must be clear. Breathing must be restored to full deep breaths instead of the quick shallow breaths associated with anxiety. Massage not only induces a more relaxed attitude, it gets the blood flowing to all the extremities. And blood flow is essential for proper sexual function and enjoyment.

I was able to achieve improved sexual response in my clients because I used a holistic approach to sex. Rather than envisioning our lives, personalities, or even our bodies as separate or distinct from our sexuality and our genitalia, I see the connections between all these aspects of existence. Although my clients might have wanted to focus on their penis or an orgasm, as an expert in my field, I encouraged them to broaden their concept of sex to include their whole body, their state of mind, and even issues from their past. If any aspect of ourselves or our lives is out of balance, it will impact our sexual function. Conversely, when you release pent-up emotions and tense muscles, sex is so much better!

If you do not have much success in convincing your partner to sit still for a massage, it may be because he believes he will have to reciprocate by giving you a massage. Some men might turn down a massage because they are simply too tired to return the favor. I recommend you pick different days to treat each other to massage. As you empower yourself to be a sexually assertive female, you will discover a great deal of satisfaction from orchestrating his pleasure. This is not unlike the satisfaction many men feel in providing women with pleasure. Unless your schedules are identical, there are probably days when you are more likely to have the energy to give him a massage and days when he has more energy to massage you.

An important ingredient to massage is breathing. I learned to incorporate breathing exercises during massage for several reasons. First, as someone who has had a lot of massages, I knew that the only way to release the tension and emotions in my body was by breathing through the massage. My massage practitioners taught me this by insisting that I breathe when I wanted to tense during the massage. I quickly realized that breathing was almost as important to the healing/rejuvenating process of massage as the touch of the massage therapist.

I had also learned how integral breath work was to male multiple orgasm techniques, and I knew that learning to control one's breathing was central to some techniques to prevent premature ejaculation. My experiences with yoga and meditation taught me that breath work was central to any efforts for relaxation or enlightenment. And, finally, by studying Tantra, I came to see how important breathing was to a sacred sexual experience.

It was only natural that I would make breathing a central feature of my encounters with my clients. So I encouraged them to relax into that first hug with a deep breath. And after I began to massage their tensions away, I gently and repeatedly reminded them to breathe deeply. If they seemed reticent to alter their shallow and tense breaths, I would invite them to breathe with me. This almost always succeeded in convincing them to stop being self-conscious and controlling and to start letting go and enjoying themselves!

Later during sex, if they had any difficulties performing sexually, I would go back to that deep breath and start over again. Employing my massage techniques to keep them focused on the physical pleasure in their body but away from their penis would often relax them enough to revive their genitals so we could resume our sex play.

Not everyone responds the same to a given massage technique. If your partner indicates that the pressure you are applying is too intense for their tastes, by all means make adjustments accordingly. However, in my experience, if I could convince a man to withstand even a couple minutes of deep tissue massage, the net impact on the sex that followed was worth it. All the methods of massage that I discuss in this chapter use more pressure than is customarily associated with eroticism.

Particularly for people who carry their emotions and daily stresses in their bodies, massage techniques seem almost necessary as a precursor to great sex. I believe that the deeper you can go in your efforts to release stress, the deeper the sexual experience and resulting orgasm(s) will be. But again, I want to emphasize that you should not spend more than 20 minutes on these massage techniques prior to sex. Otherwise, you may find your partner (and you!) are far too relaxed and drained to function sexually. A little of this goes a long way!

A lot of different types of massage are available, and some massage can leave you so relaxed or even so exhausted that you have no desire for sex. I use a variety of massage techniques for only about 10 to 20 minutes. This has the effect of relaxing the mind and body for a deeper enjoyment of sex without so completely relaxing the body that sex becomes difficult.

My favorite massage techniques when seducing a man include some acupressure, reflexology, and deep tissue, as well as breath and chakra play. Acupressure is an ancient Chinese healing method developed in Asia more than 5,000 years ago that uses the fingers to press certain points on the surface of the skin causing energy flow. By applying firm pressure to these pressure points, you can release muscular tension and improve circulation. Acupressure is like acupuncture without the needles!

Because I have had different types of acupressure treatments, I am familiar with a couple pressure points from the perspective of the patient. I did not study acupressure, and you don't need to either if you are merely interested in adding another dimension to your erotic world. However, if you want to pursue the study of acupressure for its health benefits, an excellent book on the topic is *Healing with Pressure Point Therapy* (Prentice Hall Art, 1999). In this comprehensive book, Jack Forem covers several pressure point therapies, including acupressure, shiatsu, and reflexology.

Shiatsu comes from Japan but is in fact a combination of early acupressure techniques, stretching, and chiropractic manipulations. It is one of my favorite therapeutic massages, but it has never made me think about sex. In my opinion, it is simply too extreme to transition successfully into love-making. But I highly recommend it if you simply want to stay in shape and improve your health.

Reflexology applies pressure to specific points in the feet, hands, and ears. Although the practitioners of reflexology believe that each pressure point on the foot, hand, or ear corresponds to an internal organ, you don't have to ascribe to this belief to enjoy the benefits of reflexology. I do it simply because it feels so good! You can refer to reflexology charts to pinpoint the designated pressure points, or you can do what I did and simply experiment until you find the points that feel best to you and your partner. Apply pressure with your thumb or fingertip (no fingernails) for a few deep breaths and then release. But be careful when you touch another person's feet. Most feet are very sensitive and even ticklish. I have found that a firm touch works best.

Deep tissue massage applies more pressure than sensual massage. By applying more pressure and going deeper you can release muscle tension that may have been in your partner's body for years. With this energetic release can come an emotional release. I always encouraged my clients to breathe through any discomfort and let go. If they felt like sighing or crying, that was fine, too. My objective was to assist them in releasing negative feelings so they could more fully enjoy the positive feelings of sex. Because I attempted to engage the entire person—all their hopes, dreams, fears, and frustrations—I was able to take them to places sexually that they had never been to before. I enjoyed that part of my work more than anything!

And last, but not least, you can connect with chakras. Many people do not believe chakras exist. And, yet, the concept of chakras has been with us since before 600 B.C. This is a Sanskrit term, and it is closely associated with yoga and Tantra. Coincidentally or not, the seven basic chakras correspond to the seven main nerve ganglia that emanate from the spinal column. I learned to connect with the heart chakras of my clients, which assisted me in forming an immediate and deep bond with a total stranger. In a long-term relationship, it is useful for enhancing your intimacy and connection as well.

Most of my clients thought I was nuts if I mentioned anything about chakras. It sounds so new age. This made the following demonstration all the more fun. I would align my heart chakra with his heart chakra and invite him to breathe deeply with me for a couple minutes. The heart chakra is located in the center of your chest; it is considered a "major chakra" and is a powerful emotional center. Then I would take my elbow and place it over his heart chakra and again ask him to breathe deeply with me.

Of course, my elbow did not have the same effect as my heart did. This is something most of us know intuitively without knowing why. The reason the elbow does not provide you with the same feeling of connection as the chest (heart) is simple. There is not the same energy center in the elbow as there is in the chest. Although some attribute a minor chakra to the elbow, it cannot compare to the energy generated by the heart chakra! The palm of your hand also has an energy center or chakra. You can feel more of a connection with the palm of your hand than you can with your elbow. The chakra in the palm of the hand is also usually considered a minor chakra, but some, including me, think this is incorrect.

I invite you to find out what you think. You might like to duplicate my demonstration with your partner. Experiment with the center of your chest, the palm of your hand, and your elbow. Try other body parts, too! Each time you align a given body part with a part of your partner's body, breathe deeply for a few minutes and notice what you do or don't feel. In this manner, you can both become more familiar with the subtle and not so subtle energy transfer that takes place when you hug, kiss, and touch each other. Being more aware of the energy of love and sex can only improve your love life.

You will notice that I repeatedly tap into a variety of concepts and traditions to accentuate sexuality, but spend little time expounding on the theory that may accompany it. I am the kind of person who enjoys things that get results. Why the results are obtained is of less interest to me. In this book I want to share with you the things that worked for me and the men in my life. But if you find your curiosity piqued, you may decide to explore these topics further.

A typical session for me began with that all-important heart chakra hug and deep breath. Then I had him disrobe and climb onto the massage table—face down. (If you don't have a massage table, you can use a bed or the floor, depending upon which is more comfortable for him.) I began by rubbing his back and neck with moderate pressure and then progressed to deep tissue massage on a few key muscles that seemed the most problematic. I might just massage his neck and back, or if it seemed he could use the 20-minute massage, I would work my way down his arms, legs, and buttocks. I massaged his feet and hands last. Then I moved from massage to employing pressure points. My favorite pressure points in a man include the spot between his thumb and forefinger, the back of his ankles, the arch of his foot, and a spot buried deep in the center of each buttocks cheek. You will know when you hit some of these spots based upon the way he reacts. Pressure points are powerful, so he will no doubt flinch or gasp if you contact one.

Throughout the entire process, I would remind him to breathe deeply, and I would be breathing deeply with him. My deep probing of his muscles and pressure points for 10 to 20 minutes would gradually segue into light erotic touching of his skin. Transitioning into erotic touch was an important step before beginning foreplay. I found erotic touch began to arouse the nerve endings I would be capitalizing on during foreplay and then sexual activity. This type of touch involves light strokes with your fingertips and fingernails. You want to barely connect with the skin and stroke the entire body from head to toe. Keep your touch light and your strokes slow, and you should be rewarded with quivering gooseflesh. I always waited for that physical manifestation in my partner's skin before graduating to foreplay.

Then I would slide a pillow under his hips and begin to gently stroke that little patch of skin between his rectum and his testicles (perineum). I might also play with his testicles and his rectum, or I might decide to just come dangerously close without making contact. Sometimes wanting something that never quite happens is as extremely erotic as is teasing someone to the point of distraction!

Only after all this would I allow him to roll over on his back and present his likely as not fully erect penis to me. But I would still ignore his genitals. If he seemed particularly anxious to engage in sex at this point, I would make him wait all the longer. I might conduct my little chakra demonstration, or I might give him a face and scalp massage. The point is to keep the focus off his penis for as long as possible and move into a gradual seduction with lots of foreplay. Foreplay is right around the corner—just turn the page!

17

Mastering the Art of Foreplay

Foreplay includes a wide variety of techniques intended to arouse and seduce a lover. Because we are all individuals, what may arouse one person can be a turn-off for another. This is why it is so important to pay attention to the subtle signs of pleasure, boredom, or even discomfort that your lover will give you. If you become especially skilled at reading your partner's facial expressions, rate of breathing, and sighs, you can even become aware of their desire while it is still just a subconscious feeling for them.

Most of us try to be polite, and when two people are naked and hoping for an ecstatic encounter, it can be especially difficult to be completely honest about what you like and don't like. No one wants to hurt her lover's feelings or spoil the moment. You care about this person. You are happy he desires you and wants to please you. Maybe, it's not him; maybe it's you. The temptation is to just tell him whatever he does feels good and let him think he is a great lover or hope things start feeling better in a few minutes.

The two most popular reasons to have sex are either for love or fun. If you are lying about how much you enjoy the sex, why even have sex? Obviously no one wins whenever we fake sexual pleasure or an orgasm. Apparently about 50 percent of both men and women do just that, which is sad. Certainly faking it does not do anything positive for your pleasure. And since fake is just another word for being dishonest, it also does nothing for the intimacy in your relationship. I understand how hard it can be to remain honest when everyone's clothes are off. But it really is an important requirement for good sex.

Although I encourage people to get past their inhibitions and tell the truth in a loving way, you can also work to get past your lover's less-than-candid feedback. If you are not so eager to believe that you are a wonderful lover and remain open to learning more, you can look for physical signs that your performance could use some improvement. All you have to do is refuse to settle for mediocrity and shoot for excellence!

Your lover's breathing can be a very good gauge of his level of excitement, as well as the pace at which his sexual passion is building. And your breathing can induce your lover's passion to meet yours as your sexual excitement becomes obvious with deep and perhaps audible breaths. Similarly, your lover's facial expressions will provide clues to his level of pleasure. You can increase the passion between you by gazing into his eyes and expressing your sexual excitement with your facial expressions.

Some lovemaking can be frenetic and fast-paced. Other times, lovers savor each moment and come to a slow boil. Lovers may not come together with equal levels of passion during any given interlude, but fortunately, if there is similar desire, they can find common ground on which to meet. Just be careful to look for those subtle cues and find a rhythm that is based upon the passion and mood of the moment. If your level of passion is more pronounced or faster-paced than your lover's, you can slow down a bit while encouraging him to meet your level of passion with various foreplay techniques.

Notice I am not suggesting that you use the genitals as the ultimate arbiter of sexual response. Unfortunately, the genitals often engage before our minds and hearts do. Therefore, a truly skilled lover is not checking their partner's genitals for signs of life and assuming that an erect penis is permission to jump on it. Some measure of restraint will pay off with more profound orgasms and intimacy. And even if your partner is ready and willing to skip to intercourse or oral sex, you will do both of you a big favor if you can prolong the foreplay. The amount of time and effort you put into foreplay will have a direct impact on the intensity of sex.

Some people think foreplay is largely a skill that men need to acquire in order to seduce women. Women tend to practice very little foreplay because they have been told that men are always ready and willing to have sex and don't require any warm-up. In my experience, nothing could be farther from the truth. Some men will be capable of the mechanics of sex without any foreplay, but that does not translate to a fulfilling sexual encounter. I have impressed many men with sexual outcomes that completely eclipsed their previous experiences, simply by applying foreplay techniques. Various forms of foreplay are my secret to sexual success.

The first step to mastering the art of foreplay is to empty your mind of all the stereotypes you have been taught about men, their bodies, and their sexual responses. Men and women are wired the same sexually, so, for example, nipples arouse sexual desire in everyone—not just women. And just as some women find their nipples too sensitive for direct stimulation, some men feel the same way about having their nipples touched.

However, the vast majority of men love to have their nipples directly stimulated during foreplay and sex. You can begin by flicking his nipples with your tongue. Watch for signs of pleasure such as moaning or sighing. Keep an eye on his penis for clues about the level of his sexual arousal while you try different forms of foreplay but don't touch it. Men have a tendency to focus on their penis for pleasure, and you want to engage his entire body so he will have the best orgasm ever!

Try sucking gently on his nipples and watch them become more pronounced and erect. You can also lightly pinch them with your fingers, but be careful, he may be more sensitive here than you are if he is not used to having his nipples touched. If he seems game for more, nibbling with your teeth can also be very erotic. I have had some men indicate that they want me to bite and pinch their nipples hard. If this is clearly communicated, then feel free to do so. Again, the secret to success is being sensitive to the nonverbal and verbal feedback with which your partner supplies you. If he tells you what he wants, it removes the guesswork. Most sexual interludes involve a combination of stated desires as well as desires that are never talked about.

Men also respond favorably to having their necks and ear lobes stimulated. And just as women differ as to whether they prefer licking, sucking, biting, kissing, or a combination of all four, men do, too. Some men will be positively repulsed if you stick a tongue in their ear, whereas others would follow you to the ends of the earth for more. How do you know what he prefers? Pay attention. Even if he does not say a word or offers a weak assurance that whatever you do feels good to him, you can decipher the truth.

Watch his facial expressions, listen to his breathing, and pay attention to his body language. Any tensing can be a sign that your efforts are not having the desired effect. Of course, some tension can be a good sign. So you have to look at the overall effect. If he is holding his breath and squirming with an unpleasant expression on his face, he probably doesn't like what you are doing to him. If he is breathing deeply and relaxing into your embrace with a smile on his face, you can be assured he is having a good time. Of course, most of the time his cues will be more subtle, and they may involve a combination of what appear to be signs of pleasure and discomfort, which can be confusing. If you trust your intuition while paying attention to all the nonverbal signs he is giving you, you should have little trouble discerning where his responses fall on the scale between ecstasy and disgust.

If he seems to enjoy it more than dislike it, keep it up. If he seems to hate it more than like it, do something else or change your approach. For instance, if I notice physical cues that suggest displeasure while I am tonguing a man's ear, I switch to nibbling his ear lobe. I don't interrupt the lovemaking to ask him "what's wrong?" nor do I assault his senses with a series of interrogations: "How does this feel?" "Do you like this?" and so on. I just keep fine-tuning the foreplay until I hit something that seduces him into the eroticism of the moment.

When it comes to other erogenous zones, such as the insides of the thighs and feet, I have found that men vary widely as to whether it has any effect on them at all. Very hairy men tend to have less response to light tickles on the insides of their thighs. Maybe all that hair tickles them all day, and they have learned to shut out the sensation. I don't know for certain, but I do know that I usually try to arouse the insides of the thighs even if there is a lot of hair there, but give up rather quickly if any response is lacking. Men with very little hair, however, can be extremely sensitive to light stroking of the insides of their thighs. If your man seems receptive to this type of touch, begin with your fingertips. Ever so lightly stroke the surface of the skin from his knees to his groin and back again. You can also experiment with your fingernails but again, pay attention to whether your fingertips or your fingernails seem to evoke the more pleasured response.

Feet are a special case. Some feet hate to be touched in any way. Other feet love to be adored in every way. One thing I have found to be true about feet is that most people have extreme reactions in either direction. They either can't stand to have their feet touched, or they love it! Few moderate responses exist with regard to feet. It isn't likely that you will get mixed messages from your partner about his feet. If he hates to have them touched, he will likely pull away before he even thinks about it. And if he doesn't pull away, you can be pretty confident that he will enjoy having his feet attended to in some fashion.

Even if he lets you touch his feet, don't lose sight of the fact that he may be extremely sensitive there. Begin by holding his feet like you were holding his hands. Then ever so slightly, you can test his sensitivity with gentle strokes. Be careful not to tickle. Most people are very easily tickled on their feet, and it is the rare person who finds the tickling of their feet to be erotic. Tickling other parts of your partner's body might be fun as part of foreplay. It might break some tension and add humor to the moment as long as you don't over-do it. But your ultimate intention is to create a sensuous experience. You will usually accomplish this if you avoid tickling.

As long as his feet are clean and appealing, you may want to suck his toes. Toe sucking can be very sensuous and leave your partner feeling overwrought with passion. But again, some people will not care for it. Approach your love-making like a grand experiment, taking note of those things that work and those things that don't, and you need not get your feelings hurt. Just move on to your next experiment!

After you have stimulated your man from head to toe, you can move closer to his genitals, but I encourage you to go slowly. Run your fingertips over his stomach, lick his belly button, and caress his testicles, but stay away from his penis a little longer. The sheer agony of all this anticipation is guaranteed to pay off in a big way when you finally do touch his penis. I love to work my way within fractions of an inch of his member and watch the penis do its own excited dance. You can work wonders by lightly stroking his testicles and the skin directly under his testicles. Roll him over on his stomach and put a pillow under his hips. This will give you easy access to the skin between his rectum and his testicles. This skin is also known as the perineum, and it is very sensitive to touch.

Some men will let you stroke their perineum for a very long time. It is as if they have been waiting all their life for someone to touch them there. They may lift their butts high in the air and arch their backs in ecstasy. Alternate with your fingertips and your fingernails and then switch to your tongue. The combined effect is almost guaranteed to send most men over the edge!

This is sometimes a perfect time to rim him as well. Rimming is oral-anal sex. Simply part the cheeks to his posterior and lightly run your tongue over his rectum. Our rectums have a multitude of very sensitive nerve endings in them, and this can be a source of exquisite pleasure. You may choose to do this for just a few minutes, or you may really get into it and stay longer. One thing is for sure, if you have aroused his neck, ears, nipples, thighs, belly, feet, toes, perineum, and rectum— his state of arousal will be hitting an all-time high!

18

Putting a Condom Where Your Mouth Is

I get so tired of hearing how sex can make you sick. Seems that is the only way we are allowed to talk about sex in public. We are rarely given permission to discuss as a normal part of day-to-day conversation how much fun sex is or how much we might enjoy it. But the television, radio, and magazines can blast information about sexually transmitted diseases with impunity. In fact, the diseases you can get from having sex and the possibility of pregnancy constitute the bulk of sex education in schools. Teachers who dared to talk about the pleasures associated with sex to students in grade school or even some high schools would likely risk losing their jobs. Just ask former Surgeon General Jocelyn Elders.

It's ironic, really. Food kills people every day. But even though severe food allergies and food poisoning have the ability to make people horribly sick and sometimes even kill them, we don't force restaurants to carry a warning about the potential dangers of food. We expect them to adhere to certain health and safety standards in the handling and preparation of food, but restaurant and food advertisements are all about the fun and pleasures of eating!

In the same spirit, I want to keep this book focused on the pleasures of sex instead of taking you down that tired old road of sex is dangerous and might kill you. There is so much information available about sexually transmitted infections (STIs) that I don't want to repeat it all here. Nevertheless, you do need to have some knowledge of how to stay healthy when you have sex if you are going to be able to enjoy yourself fully. You don't want any nagging fears about disease in the back of your mind while you are trying to have an orgasm.

If you are in a long-term monogamous relationship, you may think this discussion has nothing to do with you. That could be true. Or it might not be. It all depends upon how much honesty exists in your relationship. But let's assume that you don't have to worry about STIs. Believe it or not, you would still be doing yourself a big favor by learning how to incorporate latex barriers (condoms, latex gloves, dental dams, and so on) into your love life.

A first step toward having fun with latex is to buy a few items and check them out like you were inspecting a new toy. I recommend that you buy a variety of condoms, a box of latex gloves, some finger cots, a couple of dental dams, and perhaps a female condom. Be patient, I will explain what each of these is and how to use each one to amplify the pleasure quotient in your sex life!

You no doubt already know that condoms are sheaths of latex designed to fit over an erect penis. But female condoms, designed to fit inside a woman's vagina, also exist. These can be a very attractive feature for men who hate wearing condoms. Wearing a female condom also imbues some women with an increased sense of control over their bodies and their health. Obviously, since you are wearing the condom, you don't have to worry about trying to convince him to wear one. The female condom is another option in your safer sex arsenal, and you might have a lot of fun experimenting with one!

I recommend that you play with latex because it can help you to get past your curiosity and/or discomfort and begin to relate to the latex products as if they were a normal part of your sexual landscape. You can try on a glove, unroll a condom, lick a dental dam, and so on. Feel free to touch, taste, and smell each latex barrier to engage your senses. You might even test each item by rubbing it on your nipples, clitoris, and labia.

As long as you are careful not to puncture or tear your gloves, cots, or dental dams, handling them will not damage them. However, if any of your latex supplies come into contact with bodily fluids, you should discard them. They are not intended for reuse. Use them once and then throw them away.

A dental dam is simply a square of latex originally designed to help dentists isolate a tooth during a dental procedure. Someone discovered they could also be used to create a barrier for germs while performing oral-vaginal and oral-anal sex. After you experience the difference between skin-to-skin contact and skin-to-latex contact, you might be surprised to find you actually prefer the feel of latex.

I find the feel of a dental dam against my vulva to be exquisite. I also enjoy a bare tongue, but the latex is an entirely different sensual experience for me. The latex barrier actually feels more intense to me! Some people find that a drop or two of water-based lubricant on their genitals really amplifies the effect of the dental dam. The best way to find out which you prefer is to experiment with your partner. Some dental dams come flavored, so you and your partner may want to experiment with nonflavored and variously flavored versions as well.

Good sex can make it difficult to think clearly, so you might want to mark (with a pen or marker) one side of the dental dam so you know which side is for sticking (onto the vagina or anus) and which side is for licking.

Latex gloves were originally used by persons in the medical professions to protect their health while handling bodily fluids, but today lots of people wear them for a variety of reasons. Latex gloves are worn by postal workers afraid of toxic chemicals in the mail, and they are worn by hair colorists when they apply hair dyes to their clients' heads. I use latex gloves when applying self-tanner to my otherwise fair legs! You will no doubt find it handy to have a box of latex gloves around, too, and no one but your lover need know the very personal uses you have for them as well.

I wear latex gloves during sex when I want to protect myself from direct contact with seminal fluid while stimulating a man's penis with my hand and when I want to protect myself from the bacteria in the intestines while fingering his rectum. They also work well when fingering a vagina. Besides being a barrier to germs, latex gloves cover hangnails and sharp fingernails so many lovers prefer the added comfort a latex glove can afford them. If your man doesn't get a regular manicure, you may find that simply having him put on a latex glove can improve your sex life! I used to hate it if a man put his fingers inside of my vagina, but latex gloves changed my mind about that. The latex glove is smooth and silky, and if you add a couple drops of water-based lubricant, it slides right in providing all kinds of delicious sensations!

Finger cots are similar to latex gloves except they cover only one finger. If you find the latex glove too medical or sterile in appearance, a finger cot may be a nice alternative. Because they only cover one finger, they are less noticeable. Of course, you can put a finger cot on each of your fingers if you choose. Finger cots are especially handy for those pesky hang nails and jagged fingernails. Or if one of your fingers has a cut and you want to protect it from moisture and/or germs during sex play, the finger cot does the trick!

You can unwrap a few condoms to see what they look like and play with them, but keep in mind that after a condom is exposed to the air for a few hours, it will dry out and be unsafe to use during sex. It is worth it to waste a couple condoms so you can build up your comfort level while handling them. Putting a condom on a penis in an erotic fashion requires some practice. If you want to perfect your technique in private, you can purchase a dildo (silicone dildos are the best since they retain body heat, but for our purposes here rubber dildos are fine, too). Be sure to get a dildo with a base at the bottom so you can set it on a table top for ease of application. Most safer-sex instruction tells you to put a condom on with your hands. Escorts know this is the least sexy way to put a condom on, so most of us do not use our hands—we put the condom on with our mouth!

I learned to carry a newly unwrapped condom in the palm of my right hand (since I am right-handed) when I was preparing to have sex with a man. Sometimes I also hid the condom under the pillow if sex was going to take place on the bed. Every unrolled condom has two sides to it—the side that has the reservoir tip, which is a little nipple to catch the ejaculate, and the side that rolls down onto the penis. I was always careful to carry the condom so that I would be able to drop it onto an erect penis without looking at the condom first. Obviously, I wanted the side that rolls down on the penis facing out from the palm of my hand. That way all I had to do was wave my hand over the head of a man's penis and drop the condom onto it. This was quick and required no conversation about the condom.

When the condom was sitting on the head of the penis, I wasted no time rolling it down the length of the penis with my mouth. The entire operation was seamlessly incorporated into an act of oral sex—fellatio. The man rarely knew a condom was coming into play and had no opportunity to object to or protest the use of the latex barrier. In fact, I got so good at performing fellatio with a condom that more than one man jumped up in horror complaining that I had failed to put a condom on first. This helped me to realize that if you know how to do it, most men need never sacrifice pleasure while using a condom—at least not during oral sex!

The key to success with a condom during oral sex is pressure. You have to apply more pressure with your lips and tongue in order to compensate for the loss of sensation that the latex can create. Instead of focusing on light, sensual licks and flicks of your tongue, you will want to clamp your lips around his penis and push harder with your tongue. Sucking works very well, too, as this is another form of pressure. If you use this combination of techniques from the start while you are rolling the condom down the shaft of his penis, he will no doubt be so overcome with pleasurable sensations that he will not even know you have just applied a condom.

Some women may worry about deep-throating a penis. Not all of us have the same level of sensitivity or gag reflex. I do not advise women to practice deep-throating to increase their man's pleasure during oral sex. Instead, I recommend you use the pressure techniques I have just described. If you can't or don't want to roll the condom all the way down his penis with your mouth, then begin the process with your mouth and finish it with your hands. While you roll the condom down the penile shaft with your hands, be sure to continue to apply plenty of pressure and suction on the head of his penis with your mouth. The head of the penis is far more sensitive than the shaft of the penis anyway, and as long as you continue to provide ample stimulation to this part of his anatomy, he will probably have no time to wish you were going deeper with your mouth. He will be far too busy getting caught up in the ecstasy of the moment. There are many more techniques that make for a fantastic "blow job." But you will have to wait until the next chapter!

Some women love to swallow ejaculate when they perform fellatio, and some women hate it. Certainly one advantage for this latter group of women to using a condom during fellatio is that it makes it unnecessary to swallow. As you can see, whether it is hurtful hangnails or less than tasty semen, latex barriers do more than just protect you from pregnancy or disease. Latex barriers can also be a means for increasing the pleasure in your sex life!

19

Pressure, Perineum, and Play

Oral sex is a very popular and frequent sexual desire for the majority of men. No doubt this is due in part to the fact that it feels extremely good, and it allows the man to stop thinking about his sexual performance and concentrate on his sexual pleasure. Different people have different emotions about oral sex. Some women think it is dirty or disgusting, and other women simply don't find it pleasurable. However, many women truly enjoy performing fellatio and find that it turns them on. Although most men love to experience oral stimulation of their penis, some men will not allow their wives — especially the mother of their children — to perform fellatio on them.

Obviously, fellatio, as with many other sex acts, can take on meaning and metaphor that transcend the simple physical pleasure associated with the act. If you feel that performing fellatio demeans you in some way, you are less likely to want to do it. If your husband or boyfriend thinks it demeans you in some way, he may not allow you to do it. Either way, it is a rather unfortunate state of affairs when mutual sexual pleasure with the capacity to enrich our lives and increase the emotional intimacy in our relationships is thwarted by taboos. Therefore, you owe it to yourself as well as your relationship to debunk the type of thinking that leads to less fulfilling sexual sharing.

Oral sex is not any dirtier than any other kind of sex. Obviously, good hygiene increases our enjoyment of all types of sex, and it may be even more important when it comes to oral sex simply because our noses are buried in our partner's genitals. However, oral sex actually involves fewer risks to health than intercourse because our mouths contain digestive acids that can kill some germs. But don't let that lull you into a false sense of security either. Currently, the number of cases of gonorrhea of the mouth is on the increase because some people don't consider oral sex potentially dangerous to their health. The point is that you should take precautions no matter where you are putting the penis—your mouth, vagina, or rectum. But it certainly doesn't make any logical sense to eliminate oral sex from your sex life because you think it is dirty. Oral sex is just as clean as any other form of sex.

Some women love the taste of male ejaculate, and some women can't stand it. A woman's preference can also vary from man to man since the semen of one man will taste different from the semen of another man. If you don't like the taste of semen or have any other reservations to tasting or swallowing ejaculate, you need not let that prevent you from becoming proficient at performing fellatio. Now that you know how to perform an amazing blow job with a condom (I covered this in the last chapter, remember?), you can simply eliminate any risk of a distasteful experience. If you don't like the taste of your man's ejaculate, a condom will catch it for you so you don't have to taste or swallow it. Meanwhile, you just added another hot sexual activity for the two of you to share!

As a courtesan, I learned that I never have to do anything I don't want to do—ever! The power of choice gave me permission to enjoy fellatio for the first time in my life. Because I would only go as deep as I wanted to, only do it for as long as I wanted to, and only do it *if* I wanted to, I was able to stop feeling like I was in a tug-of-war for control of the bedroom (and my body) and simply focus on sexual pleasure. Sometimes my pleasure came from watching his pleasurable responses; sometimes my pleasure resulted from my own erotic connection to the act of performing fellatio; and sometimes I enjoyed it for both reasons.

Some women love fellatio because it is a form of oral gratification. You get to lick, suck, and swallow just like you do some of your favorite foods. It might even remind you of an ice cream cone or some other delicious dessert. Of course, for those women who do not feel this way about fellatio, the very idea that other women may find it that much of a turn-on will no doubt seem preposterous. Nevertheless, this only highlights the great diversity of perceptions and experiences that exist when it comes to sex.

I have found that taking an active and assertive role with fellatio—as with any other form of sex—can greatly increase my ability to enjoy it. In addition, fellatio can be performed from a variety of positions, and you may find that you prefer some over others. Pay attention to your own feelings when you perform in these different positions, and you will find out what works for you and what doesn't.

Fellatio is something that can be conveniently conducted in a variety of settings. I have found it extremely naughty fun to give my partner a blow job in the office, in the car, in the bathroom (there are laws against sex in public bathrooms), in the woods while camping, and so on. Since the man can be sitting, standing, or lying down while getting a blow job, just about any private location will work.

Some movies hint at the idea of performing fellatio while the man is driving a car. I don't recommend this, as it is a safety hazard. Not only can the pleasure and orgasm distract the man so that he can't concentrate on his driving, but if you get into a fender bender, he could sustain some major damage to his penis in the course of the accident. It would be a sad ending to an otherwise playful interlude. If you like making out in automobiles, leave the car parked in the garage with the engine off. That way you not only ensure your safety, but you won't be exposing others to your sexual display. Most states have laws against public forms of sex, so be advised.

The most common position for fellatio is with the man lying on his back and the woman kneeling over his genitals. This is probably the most comfortable position for the man since he has only to lay back, relax, and let the good times begin. It also affords you a lot of maneuverability since you are on top. However, if you have long hair, it can be annoying if your hair is constantly falling into your face and possibly getting into your mouth. You might want to consider a hair pin or hair comb to hold your hair out of your face while you are giving him "head." This also has the added benefit of allowing him to watch. Many men love to see their penis glide in and out of your mouth as it creates even more sexual excitement for them.

Both you and your partner can stimulate each other simultaneously in the position known as the 69. As stated in previous chapters, a 69 positions your mouth over your lover's genitals while his mouth is over your genitals. You literally assume the position of the six and nine in the number 69. Some people love this position because both sexual participants not only give pleasure but receive pleasure at the same time. However, others find it distracting to give oral sex and get oral sex at the same time. For these individuals, it makes more sense to take turns so each of you can concentrate on what you are doing and/or feeling. While in a 69, you can take turns being on the top or the bottom, and you can also lie beside each other.

My favorite position for fellatio is with the man standing. I begin by asking him to stand still while sideways to a full length mirror. Immediately, most men will feel a surge of excitement wondering what the mirror is for and why they have to stand still. I have never met a man who won't comply with this request, however. Depending upon his stage of undress, you can take this opportunity to slowly undress him, beginning with the buttons on his shirt, proceeding to his belt and pants, and finishing with his shoes and socks. If he tries to assist you, insist that he doesn't. It is much more erotic to be undressed than to take off your own clothes.

After he is naked, you will want to be sure to pay some attention to his neck and nipples before you descend to his penis with your mouth. If you are using a condom, be sure to put it on with your mouth. With or without a condom, as you go down on him, you can continue to stimulate his nipples with your fingers as you slide down the length of his body. When he sees himself in the mirror, naked and erect while you engulf his penis with your mouth, he will think he has died and gone to heaven.

But there is so much more to do to make this the best oral sex he has ever had! There is a little patch of skin between his testicles and his anus called the perineum; I have mentioned it before. It is extremely sensitive to touch and can amplify the pleasurable effects of any stimulation of the penis. You can experiment by stroking the perineum lightly first with your fingertips and then your fingernails. Gently pushing the perineum also feels good to most men. This area is identified as both a chakra (energy center for meditation) and a pressure point (for acupressure). It is also where the base of the penis resides. The skin itself is very sensitive to touch. So whether you stroke it lightly or apply a fair amount of pressure, you will be sure to elicit his approval.

Don't forget to stimulate his testicles as well. This can be accomplished by licking them, sucking them into your mouth one at a time, as well as stroking them with your fingertips and fingernails. Testicles are quite sensitive, so be careful. Every man has a different threshold of pain and pleasure so be sure to pay attention to his nonverbal cues; tensing or pulling away can indicate displeasure while heavy breathing and moving toward the stimulation tells you he is having a good time.

Because not all men are the same, don't assume you know what he does and doesn't like. I have found that some men prefer a light touch, but others want to be touched roughly. Although one man might adore having the crown of his penis licked tenderly, another may find that far too subtle. He may want you to handle his penis firmly and use lots of pressure with your mouth and tongue. Most men have the majority of their sensation in the upper portion of their penis, but they will also want you to stimulate the entire length of their penis part of the time.

If you don't like going deep with your mouth, you can use your hand to grasp the shaft of his penis while you continue to suck the head of his penis with your mouth. In fact, holding the base of the penis with your hand during fellatio can have an added benefit. If, for any reason, his penis is not as erect as you want it to be, holding the base of his penis firmly will correct the problem in most cases. This operates from the same principle as a *cock ring*, which is a little ring that is placed around the base of the penis. It holds the blood in the penis facilitating an erection. Certainly your warm hand is an even sexier way to accomplish this!

Some men will prefer a particular side of the penis, too. The frenulum (the patch of skin on the crown of the penis facing away from the man's belly when his penis is erect) is a favorite for most men. The frenulum is easy for you to reach with your tongue while performing fellatio because it is right in front. I usually use light flicks of my tongue here since it tends to be more sensitive than other portions of the penis.

I have learned to use my mouth and both hands simultaneously while performing fellatio. While I alternate between light and firm, deep and shallow, fast and slow movements with my tongue and mouth, I will have one hand on his perineum and the other on his nipple. Or, I may put a finger on his perineum while I hold his testicles firmly in my other hand. The idea is to provide so many sensations that he is blown away! In addition to all of these wonderful erogenous zones—the frenulum, perineum, testicles, the base of the penile shaft, and the nipples—there is one more extremely potent part of a man's body that you can stimulate during fellatio. I tell you all about it in Chapter 22 where you will learn one more advanced technique for creating perfect fellatio. So read on!

20

Male Multiple Orgasms

Most of us have been told that only women can have multiple orgasms. I am here to tell you that is a myth. Men *can* and *do* experience multiple orgasms—several orgasms without a rest period in between the orgasms—just like women do. Most men who achieve multiple orgasms do so by *not* ejaculating when they have an orgasm. They may have an ejaculation with the last orgasm, or they may not ejaculate at all. The man who has learned to have multiple orgasms—and it does in fact require some practice for most men to achieve—has also taken his sexual awareness and enjoyment to a whole new level. How do I know? I have seen it several times with my own eyes.

Regardless of what the doctors or the books may say—and they don't agree with each other on this matter—firsthand experience can be the best source of information at times. Certainly given the diversity of sexual responses that is possible, my exposure to many male bodies in the throes of sexual ecstasy has its advantages. I might never have believed that male multiple orgasms were possible if I hadn't seen it myself. Certainly, we all know a man might be able to recover from his orgasm more quickly than usual on some occasions and thereby have an orgasm several times in one night. But multiple orgasm is about having a series of orgasms one after the other without a rest or recovery period in between orgasms.

Learning how to achieve male multiple orgasm involves knowing how to use the pubococcygeus or PC muscles (remember those from Chapter 8?) in conjunction with controlling your breathing. Obviously, this is something your man will need to take an active interest in if he is going to learn how to do it. But you can encourage him by first letting him know it is physically possible for him, and second, by pointing the way for him to learn more about it (this chapter is a good place to start).

Why should you care whether he experiences multiple orgasms or not? Well, technically, it may not make that much difference in your level of sexual enjoyment. But you can derive a great deal of pleasure from watching your man experience pleasure. The other benefit to you is the fact that men who develop this ability tend to put a lot more effort into sex in general, which means he is more likely to perfect his lovemaking skills as well. When he becomes adept at having orgasms without ejaculating, he may also be able to sustain an erection longer, which has obvious appeal to most women.

While you are exploring your sexual responses and those of your partner, you should never lose sight of an important guideline: Sex is *not* a competition. That may seem a simple truth, but in fact, it can be rather difficult to make sure you don't let your sex life become a contest. We live in a very competitive society, and the media constantly bombards us with messages about our imagined inadequacies. Men have a long history of sexual performance concerns that can range from mild to severe. A mild case of performance anxiety might mean he is so busy trying to impress his lady with his prowess that he reduces his own level of enjoyment. A severe case of performance anxiety can mean he is unable to sustain an erection or ejaculate at all.

Women can also suffer from feelings of inadequacy when it comes to their sexual function. Although most women are not so concerned with performing sexually, they can be made to feel insecure if they think they should know how to female ejaculate, have multiple orgasms, and so on. One of the risks of discovering that as humans we have this almost limitless capacity for increased sexual pleasure, is that we can feel we should have the biggest and best orgasms. There is no "should" when it comes to your sex life. All that matters is that you and your partner are happy.

Although some orgasms may feel more overwhelming than others, all sexual pleasure is satisfying on some level, so don't allow yourself to focus on what might have been when you could be enjoying what is. In other words, experiment and learn about sex with an eye for increasing your enjoyment and intimacy, but remain appreciative for what you already have. That way, you will be open to new levels of sexual joy without creating a mental hierarchy or oppressive goal, both of which can lead to frustration and disappointment. In addition, whenever you are performance-oriented, you have way too much of your energy and focus in your head, which can prevent physical pleasure. Exploring sex with the playful attitude of a child will go a long way in keeping things fun and enabling you to experience new sexual sensations.

If you maintain an attitude of curiosity and approach your sexual experimentation with some detachment, you will have more fun than if you aggressively pursue your sexual goals as if you are trying to win. Sex does not work very well if you are trying. It works a lot better if you let go.

That said, you may find experimenting with your guy's ability to orgasm to be a lot of fun. I have been amazed at the diversity among men. I have met men who can ejaculate without an erection, men who can have an orgasm without ejaculating, men who can maintain an erection throughout several orgasms, and men who can stay hard throughout several ejaculations. It helps to separate ejaculation and orgasm in your mind. Although they often occur simultaneously in male sexual response, they are not the same thing. Ejaculation is the emission of semen in males and seminal-like fluid in females. Orgasms can occur in both men and women as something separate and distinct from ejaculation. I will discuss female ejaculation in further detail in Chapter 23.

Men who already knew how to achieve multiple orgasms taught me about male multiple orgasm. I took what I learned from them; added some technical information from books, tapes, and websites; and transferred that information to other men. I had a lot of fun teaching men about male multiple orgasms. Most men do not think they are physically equipped for it, so it comes as a tantalizing surprise to learn otherwise. I like being the bearer of good news! And since I was informed as to how men can achieve multiple orgasms, I could pass that information on to the men I saw as an escort. I encourage you to become an erotic expert in your own relationship and take the initiative to teach new paths to pleasure whenever you get the opportunity. If you show an interest and a willingness to watch him while he practices, this can also become another way for you to share sexually.

I have witnessed several men attain multiple orgasms, and none of them got there in exactly the same fashion. So although there are authors who proclaim that their method for male multiple orgasms is the one right way to do it, my experience has taught me that different men respond to different techniques. I have also noticed that quite a few men have multiple orgasms and don't know it. Since these men have been told all their lives that ejaculation and orgasm are one and the same, they become terribly confused when they feel an orgasm but see no semen. The typical response is "I thought I came, but I must not have." I believe you should trust your feelings. If you feel like you had an orgasm, you did.

Men who pursue multiple orgasms consciously usually use some combination of breath control, PC muscle control, vocalizations, and repeatedly stopping and starting stimulation before ejaculation occurs. I have also seen quite a few men achieve multiple orgasms with or without an erection by applying a vibrator to the base of their penis. As you will discover in Chapter 22, men are also capable of mind-blowing internal orgasms (singular or multiple) when they are stimulated anally. In Chapter 21, I discuss orgasms resulting from Tantric breathing absent of any genital stimulation. Tantric orgasms can also occur in multiples. So as you can see, there really is no limit to the ways in which men can experience sexual pleasure. They have just as much capacity for it as women do.

If your man is not already experiencing multiple orgasms and he decides that he would like to, you can share the following techniques with him and help him practice! First, he needs to become familiar with his PC muscles. Just as with women, the best way to locate your PC muscles is by starting and stopping the flow of your urine. After you are familiar with the muscles, you can practice squeezing and relaxing them while sitting at your desk or while driving your car in commuter traffic. It is a wonderful exercise for both men and women with the power to improve your sex life on many levels: stronger erections, increased control of ejaculation, a tighter vagina, and more intense orgasms.

After a man knows how to flex his PC muscles, he can apply that ability while masturbating in order to achieve multiple orgasms. As he feels himself getting to the point of ejaculating, he should stop masturbating, squeeze his PC muscles, take a deep breath for about 10 seconds, and then continue to masturbate. If this technique works for him, he will experience an orgasm while preventing an ejaculation. He can then continue to stimulate himself (or you can help him) until he experiences another orgasm. As he masters this technique, he can begin to use it while he is having sex with you. Then the two of you can have sex for a longer period of time and share the bliss of multiple orgasms.

Notice, however, that this technique uses holding your breath. This works for some men. But others breathe through their orgasm rather than hold their breath. Breathing and vocalizing can turn masturbation into more of a meditation and engage the entire body and mind, not just the genitals. The sexual energy can be redirected through a specific sort of vocalization some refer to as "roaring" or finding "your key sound."

Male multiple orgasm techniques that use sound are similar to Tantric sex because they utilize breathing and a more meditative or spiritual approach to sex. Some people liken the roar or key sound to a meditation mantra (words and/or sounds that are repeated). You can learn more about the key sound technique, which was perfected by Jack Johnston, if you listen to "Male Multiple Orgasm: Step-by-Step" (audio CD ISBN: 1882899067).

The first time I saw a man achieve multiple orgasms, I was a little surprised at how much noise he made. Many men seem to experience orgasms without making a lot of noise. In fact we tend to associate screaming and other loud noises with female sexual response. But men who have mastered the male multiple orgasm seem to share an uninhibited enjoyment of their sexual peaks. They breathe hard, gasp, roar, moan, and even scream. After you get past any initial surprise, you might find this vocal display of arousal in men very sexy.

Having watched various men use all of the techniques for male multiple orgasm at one time or another, I don't think one method is more effective than another. Instead, I think every man is an individual and what might work for one man is not necessarily going to work for the next man. That's why it is important in the quest for more sexual pleasure to be open to some experimentation. Try all of these techniques until you discover which one(s) work best for you and your partner.

Fortunately, the very fact that information has expanded your concept of what is possible will propel your sex life into new territory to some degree. Who knows, next time you are having sex, you and your partner may find you are aware of orgasms you didn't even know you were having. Part of the process of amplifying sexual enjoyment involves merely slowing down to "smell the roses" as the saying goes. In other words, your body and your partner's body are more like untapped resources than ineptitude waiting to be trained. If you simply pay attention, you will find more joy.

21

Breathing Life into Sex with Tantra

I have already talked about the importance of deep breathing to achieve a full sexual experience. Any time you are holding your breath or breathing shallow breaths, you are not accessing the full array of sensuality of which your body is capable. Full, deep breathing facilitates a fuller sexual experience. Conscious breathing, which simply means having an awareness of your breathing, also helps to bring your energy and your concentration out of your head and into your body.

In this chapter we will explore this concept further with a brief study in Tantric sex. Tantric sex uses breathing techniques to intensify intimacy as well as orgasms. Tantra is a spiritual path that acknowledges the connection or wholeness of sex and spirit, and spirit and flesh. As such, the breath becomes a focal point because it is in the act of breathing that we unite spirit with flesh. Tantra has received the most attention in Western cultures as it applies to sexual practice. However, Tantra is not just about sex; it encourages letting go and feeling your oneness with everything. This probably sounds exotic and perhaps unattainable for the average person. But, in fact, you probably practice some Tantra today and just don't know it.

Tantric sex brings the physical sex act into unison with spiritual enlightenment. Although some will tell you this is best accomplished in the context of a long-term monogamous relationship, I can attest to the fact that Tantra has the potential to transform any sexual encounter into a spiritually imbued event. By bringing elements of meditation into sexual practice, you can begin to see the transformative power of sex. I have attained extremely meaningful and emotionally intense connections with my clients through Tantric sex. So I know firsthand that if your intention is to create space for a sacred sexual interaction, you can do so no matter who you are with. In fact, your partner need not be convinced of nor experienced in Tantra or other spiritual sexual practices to enable you to transform the sex act into an enlightening union.

The first time I ever consciously experienced Tantric sex, I was taking a class called Fire Breath Orgasm. It was taught by a very accomplished Tantra priestess named Jwala. I and about 25 other women lay on the floor of a large dimly lit room fully clothed. Our knees were bent, and our feet were flat on the floor. Our hands were at our sides and never even once did we touch ourselves or each other. Jwala instructed us to contract our PC muscles (pubococcygeus—please see Chapter 8 for more details) as we breathed in through our nose. After a long deep breath and an intense squeeze of our PC muscles, we were to simultaneously exhale and relax. At first it seemed a bit awkward. But in just a few minutes I was actually enjoying the rhythmic and meditative qualities of this exercise. But it did not feel sexual to me in the least.

One by one the women in the room began to make orgasmic sounds. Because I wasn't feeling a thing except a little dizzy, I thought they were faking it. When the entire room began to moan and scream with ecstatic erotic fulfillment, I knew it must be a case of mass-induced hysteria. How could anyone feel that good with their clothes on and their hands at their sides? The idea was ridiculous to me. But I am a scientist at heart, so I persisted with the exercise—breathing, contracting, and thinking all the while what a bunch of nonsense this whole thing was.

About 20 minutes into this exercise and after everyone else in the room had reached an orgasmic high that had them reeling with joy and excitement, I was ready to quit. I thought I would just lie about how wonderful it was, tell my teacher thanks, and get out of there as quickly as possible. While I was mapping my escape from this increasingly uncomfortable situation, my body was still breathing, contracting, and relaxing. Suddenly, I felt a burst of energy I could only describe as electric. It began at the base of my spine and shot up and out of the top of my head. It was hot like fire. And in that moment, I felt oneness with the universe and my concept of God.

My genitals didn't feel a thing. This was an entirely new kind of sex that was at first difficult for me to understand. A peacefulness and joy came over me. And I began to comprehend another dimension to sexuality. It became apparent to me that our current definitions are too narrow to encompass all that sex is. Sex is the creative spark that begets life, and it is a doorway to joy and oneness. In my opinion, it is also a gateway to the divine.

I took more Tantra classes after this one. I learned how one's breathing can affect all facets of life, not just sex. I learned to use my breathing to connect to my intuition and the hearts of others. This was an invaluable tool for me as an escort. The first thing I would do when I met a new client was give him a hug. And while I was hugging him, I would breathe deeply and align my heart chakra with his (see Chapter 16 for more about chakras). It would only take a couple seconds for me to ascertain the man's energy. Was he kind or afraid? Warm or distant? Available for intimacy or guarded and controlling?

It may seem incredible to think you can tell all of that from a simple hug. But, in fact, you probably already employ elements of this in your life. Next time you hug someone, just take a minute to breath into the hug and feel the flow of energy. That energy has always been there, and you are no doubt already accessing the information on some level. I am simply encouraging you to become more conscious of this normal day-to-day experience. If you become more aware of the energy between you and others, you will no doubt be able to make better assessments about social situations, and you will be able to channel more intense sexual energy when you desire to do so.

Far more information reaches our brains than we are consciously aware of. Body language and smell are two cues that give us a great deal of information about others; however, we are usually consciously focused on the words and overt behavior of others instead. Thankfully, the more subtle cues still reach our brains, and we often make decisions based upon a combination of all these information sources. Learning to relax into my breathing helped me clear my mind of prejudice and fear so that I could feel the energy of another person with an open heart and an open mind. This is something we have all done from time to time. Tantra just taught me to do it intentionally and regularly by consciously focusing on my breathing.

In addition, my knowledge of Tantric breathing enabled me to alter my clients' states of mind and emotions so I could improve the sexual encounters. By encouraging them to breathe into a hug, a massage, and/or a sexual embrace, I was able to reduce their anxiety, tension, and stressful thoughts. Since sex is best when we can let go and stop thinking, Tantric breathing is a wonderful way to redirect our attention and allow ourselves a fuller sexual experience.

So aside from a novel way to masturbate, Tantra can add a spiritual dimension to sex with another person. It deepens the connection while releasing more intense emotions. For many, this also translates to improved sexual function. Tantric breathing can also prolong the sexual experience, as well as the resulting orgasms. If you and your partner practice Tantric breath during sex, your connection and your erotic experience will find new depth and meaning as well as new highs in sexual performance. Most importantly, Tantra can assist you in incorporating a spiritual dimension to your lovemaking, thereby creating more sexual wholeness.

Teaching Tantra is beyond the scope of this book, so I recommend that you sign up for a class or two and find out whether it resonates with you. If I had merely read a book, I would never have become convinced of the power of Tantra. It really is something that has to be experienced to be appreciated, and talking about it just creates more questions than answers. You might begin your journey online at www.tantra.com. This comprehensive website contains free resources, as well as a membership section and a well-stocked Tantric store. Who knows, perhaps you will decide to order a video or DVD such as *Tantric Lovemaking*. I recommend that you give yourself an opportunity to see Tantra in action before you decide whether it is for you or not. If I had not done so myself, I would still think it was silly. And I would have cheated myself out of an extremely rich sex life.

22

His Prostate Pleasure

Male clients ask for this, hint about this, and sometimes just quietly hope for this. Anal stimulation in one form or another is such a popular request that escorts really can't expect to be in business without offering some form of it. Of course, escorts don't know this when they begin their new profession. No one tells us in advance, so we learn as we go.

When a group of escorts get together, the conversation invariably turns to this particular male preoccupation. We whisper about it over lunch. We joke about it. We refer to it in short hand. We laugh and giggle with knowing smiles. I think many of us are surprised by the frequency with which we get requests for some kind of anal stimulation. Most escorts agree that it is the most often requested sex act, second only to the blow job.

Anal stimulation can take many different forms. Rimming, prostate massage, butt plug play, and penetration with a strap-on dildo are all forms of anal sex that a female can perform on a male. If you don't know exactly what these techniques are or involve, read on as I will describe each one in this chapter.

The pay-offs for anal stimulation are also potentially high. For men, this often can be the only way they will ever experience orgasms that are as intense and full body as the orgasms they have been watching their female partners have over the years. Many men are actually quite jealous of the orgasmic potential of women and long to feel sexual pleasure that is internal and overwhelming. Over the years, I have witnessed thousands of male orgasms, and some barely rivaled the physical magnitude of a sneeze. However, with anal penetration, I have seen men completely overcome with pleasurable sensation, which has often culminated in an emotional release as well. Tears of joy are not required, but also are not uncommon for the man who has his first anally aroused orgasm.

There is some controversy about the mechanics of anal stimulation. Certainly, all agree that the sphincter muscle that guards the entrance to the anus is packed full of sensitive nerve endings that can produce enormous pleasure sensations if lightly stroked or licked. But regarding the pleasures of penetration, some refer to the spot that feels the best in males as the prostate and some call it the G-spot.

Most physicians barely acknowledge a female G-spot, so there is no way you are going to get them to admit to a male G-spot. However, it is an established medical fact that all men have a prostate gland. The prostate gland produces sperm and seminal fluid. The female G-spot is thought to be analogous to the prostate because it produces a fluid chemically similar to male seminal fluid.

As a sex worker with more hands-on experience than most of these folks in lab coats, I can only tell you that it doesn't really matter what you call it, stimulation of that spot (G or otherwise) in a male produces an intense inner orgasm usually accompanied by ejaculation of some type of fluid. There are exceptions, of course, but I have found that almost all men feel something when their G-spot is stimulated. Some don't enjoy the sensation or experience it as too intense. But most find it a source of pleasure. I suspect that the G-spot is a patch of erectile tissue located similarly in both males and females, lying in front of either the prostate in males or paraurethral glands (also called Skene's Glands) in females. The proximity to these glands could explain why stimulation usually results in ejaculation.

However, current medical literature insists that anal penetration of males applies pressure to the prostate gland and that all the sexual pleasure associated with penetration of males is due to the prostate gland. Of course, it matters little whether you call it the prostate or the G-spot; what is important is that it feels very good and is even good for you!

Risks are associated with any kind of anal play, and you must be fully aware of these before you initiate any type of anal sex. As an escort, I learned how to perfect numerous forms of anal play, and each can be performed quite safely. It is very important to play safe with any kind of sex, but doubly so with anal sex. The risk of transmitting STIs and AIDS is much higher with anal play because there are so many tiny blood vessels at the surface of the intestines. These blood vessels can be easily broken and provide a route of entry for disease without any visible blood.

The more obvious risk is associated with the bacteria that live in the intestines and rectal area. These bacteria can cause infection and disease if they come into contact with vaginas, urethras, open wounds, mouths, or food. The best way to prevent problems is to use a latex glove on your hand and a condom on any toys being inserted into the anus. I prefer to use condoms on my dildos no matter what orifice they are stimulating. I still wash the dildo after every use, but using a condom offers another layer of protection and disease prevention.

You can protect yourself during oral-anal contact such as rimming by using a dental dam (small latex squares used by dentists during dental procedures). Latex gloves and condoms can also be cut open and used just like a dental dam.

If you use a dildo, it is important that you use one that is specifically intended for anal stimulation. Dildos designed for vaginal fun are typically too big for anal comfort in many beginners, and most importantly, they have no flange. Anal probes or butt plugs have a flange at one end to prevent them from getting sucked up into your rectum. There is nothing more embarrassing than a trip to the emergency room to get something retrieved from your rectum.

Because the large intestine is about 5 feet long and the small intestines can be up to 30 feet in length, objects that get lost can wind up working their way into the digestive tract, causing a life-threatening obstruction. Some people have actually died because they used inappropriate objects as anal sex toys, so make sure you are informed and proceed with due caution.

Lube is an important consideration for anal play of any kind. The rectum is not lubricated naturally no matter how much sexual arousal may exist, so lubrication must be supplied artificially. If you intend to use latex of any kind, including but not limited to condoms, you must use a water-based lubricant.

Any kind of oil or petroleum jelly will cause the latex to degrade, thereby affording you less, if not zero, protection.

In addition, the rectum is designed to absorb nutrients, so it does a marvelous job of absorbing lubricant. You will need to replenish it frequently. By keeping the anus lubricated, you can minimize any microscopic tears that may occur from anal sex play and consequently reduce the risk of disease transmission. It also feels better when you use generous amounts of lubrication.

Now that we have covered the safer sex considerations, you are ready to begin anal play. It is preferable to begin by using your fingers because this will provide you with valuable information about your partner's preferences—information that you will use for all other play. Nothing will be quite as personal or provide as much tangible feedback as inserting your fingers into his rectum. You will be able to feel him tense, relax, breathe, contract, and finally orgasm. This intimate experience may be emotionally moving for you as well as him.

Penetrating another person requires us to be responsible and responsive. It is an act of trust and vulnerability from the person who allows us to penetrate them. For this reason, this type of sexual intimacy can add a particularly deep and meaningful dimension to relationships.

You will eventually discover the details that work for you and your partner, but to begin with, you may want to copy my routine for introducing a man to anal penetration. Rimming, encircling the outer rim of the anus with your tongue, is a nice way to start because tongues are less threatening than fingers or toys. I never rimmed my clients without a latex barrier. I have rimmed my husband bareback and have found it quite erotic as long as he was freshly showered. Rimming is pretty straight-forward. Simply spread your lover's cheeks and begin gently licking his anus. If he seems to like the sensation, you can experiment further with more vigorous tongue action, including inserting your tongue further into his rectum. Of course, you may decide not to insert your tongue as a personal preference. If both of you desire deeper insertion, this is a good time to begin finger play.

I like to lay the man on his back with his knees bent and his legs slightly spread. I put a towel under his buttocks to protect the sheets. As I put the latex glove onto my right hand (the glove not only protects us from disease, it protects his rectum from my fingernails), I usually smile and crack a little joke such as "Dr. Monet to the rescue," which is not all that funny but evokes a little chuckle just the same because of the man's nervous tension. Laughter relaxes the sphincter muscle, so with my corny joke I am preparing him for what is to come.

I apply a generous amount of lube to my index finger and gently rub it around his anus and perineum. This feels wonderful for the man and relaxes him further. He will usually try to anticipate when I am going to insert my finger, and I try to linger at the entrance long enough to catch him off guard. Then I carefully and slowly dip my finger about a half inch into his rectum. The sphincter muscle tightens around my finger, and if I stay there and don't penetrate further, he is likely to feel more like defecating and less like having sex. So I push a little deeper and feel the second sphincter muscle close around my finger. This muscle cannot be relaxed consciously, so if he feels the least bit of pain and indicates he wants to stop, I will back off for a while and return to playing around the rim of his rectum.

It is important to proceed further only if the man indicates that he is still interested. If he is feeling too anxious, the second sphincter muscle will be so tight that penetration will cause a great deal of pain for most people. It would be better to wait until he is more relaxed and open to the idea at another time than risk turning him off to anal play entirely. When he indicates that he wants to be penetrated deeper, you can insert your index finger all the way in. Make sure that you cup your hand toward his belly so that once you are inside of him, your finger will be hitting his G-spot or prostate.

Ever so slowly at first, move your index finger to make the "come here" motion. You will feel a depression in the wall of his rectum that falls almost exactly where your index finger ends if it is completely inserted. In my experience, this area becomes more erect or engorged the more I play with it. This is why I prefer to call it the male G-spot.

Experiment with light stroking as well as more pressure. Encourage him to let you know which motion and pressure feels best to him. You can stimulate him in this manner without using any other sexual techniques, or you can add other sex play to enhance the experience.

For example, during prostate massage or any other kind of anal sex, massaging the perineum can increase the pleasure factor exponentially! The perineum is located between the anus and the genitals of either sex. It is rich in nerve endings and considered a chakra as well as an acupressure point in Eastern meditation and medicine. As you will notice throughout this book, I use this tiny patch of skin during all kinds of sexual activity.

If you prefer, there are prostate massagers designed to stimulate the perineum while they massage the prostate. High Island Health (www.highisland.com) offers several models. But you don't have to buy any special equipment to stimulate your partner's perineum. Just touch the area with your finger. Vary the pressure from a light tickle to a deep massage and watch his face, body language, breathing, and erection for feedback. You will quickly discover what type of touch he prefers. In fact, this form of feedback can sometimes provide you with more accurate information than asking him how he feels or what he wants. Most men have difficulty expressing themselves under ordinary circumstances, but they are doubly incapacitated when the topic is sexual. Sexual response will usually lead the way to sexual satisfaction, even when verbal communication is less than informative.

I usually like to add at least one other sexual technique while massaging the prostate, which can also have the effect of distracting him so he relaxes further. While my right index finger is still in his anus, I use my mouth and/or my left hand to arouse his nipples, massage his perineum, or stimulate his penis.

If you arouse at least two erogenous zones simultaneously, most men will reach orgasm fairly quickly, so if you want to slow the process down, just stop moving your index finger for a few beats while holding your place on his prostate. Then when you resume stimulation of this area, the resulting orgasm will be just that much more satisfying. As he orgasms, you will feel the waves of pleasure inside of him. Do not remove your finger during the orgasm or even right afterward. Stay inside of him and hold him and/or comfort him if it seems appropriate.

As stated before, many men will cry or feel some form of deep emotion when they have an internal orgasm, especially if it is their first. Try to treat him the way you would want to be treated at such a time. If you suddenly yank your finger out of him, you risk creating feelings of abandonment and emptiness. You will also miss the power and intensity of his orgasm. For me, this was always a sacred sexual moment for which I wanted to be fully present.

If you decide you want to experiment further, you can graduate to anal toys. It is best to make your first anal toy a smallish butt plug. You have plenty of time to work your way up to the larger toys if you feel so motivated. For example, you may want to try a strap-on sooner rather than later. Using a strap-on in a heterosexual context has recently become quite popular as evidenced by adult videos such as the *Bend Over Boyfriend* series produced by SIR Video Productions (www.sirvideo. com/bob.html).

It is best to go shopping for your strap-on as a couple. If he's like most men, your partner will want to select the dildo that is going to be inserted into him to make sure it is not too big nor too small depending upon his particular tastes. You will want to make sure the strap-on device suits your fancy and fits you properly. Be sure to test the equipment before you take it home simply by making sure the dildo fits securely into the strap-on and won't fly out during passionate lovemaking. And don't forget to buy lots of lube. You will need more of it for strap-on play than you did for finger play simply because the surface of any dildo is larger than the surface of your finger.

A strap-on gives you an opportunity to do a little role reversal and find out what it might feel like to have a penis. Unlike a real penis, your dildo will not provide you with physical sensation, but you can purchase a strap-on harness with a pocket for a vibrator that fits at the base of the dildo and stimulates your clitoris. Harnesses come in a variety of styles. I found one online (www.goodvibes.com) that looks like a corset!

You can have a lot of fun trying different positions with your new toy. He can sit on top of you. You can enter him from behind, or lay him on his back and have him put his legs up over your shoulders. If he is really into the role reversal, you can even pretend that he is giving you a blow job. I have had more than one heterosexual client really get into this kind of fantasy play. Of course, many men would find that to be a turn-off, so as with all things sexual, you need to take it on an individual basis. What one person finds hot can leave another cold.

Remember to go slowly and be responsive to the feedback your partner gives you—verbal as well as nonverbal. I have occasionally gotten so into what I was doing that I neglected the subtle cues my partner was giving me about his level of enjoyment. It is doubly important that you pay attention when you are in the driver's seat, so to speak. Depending upon your partner's particular preferences and even his mood, he may prefer something gentle and slow, something fast and furious, or something in between. The same applies to the depth of penetration. Some men prefer shallow penetration, but others want it as deep as possible. Be sure to keep the communication lines open so you both have a good time.

Some men are terrified of experiencing any anal pleasure. They are usually afraid that if they enjoy any kind of rimming or penetration of their rectum, this might mean they are gay.

These are usually the poor chaps who are also too paranoid to allow their bodies to feel pleasure via their nipples. And true to form, this kind of rigid sexuality has the habit of resulting in some very unremarkable orgasms. A barely perceptible sigh or groan, and it's all over.

Fortunately, most men are way too pleasure-oriented to worry whether the sex police think it's proper. If it feels good … do it! In fact, the most impressive male orgasms I have been witness to have occurred through anal stimulation. The male body responds in totality. Waves of pleasure travel throughout the entire body in response to some very powerful contractions in the rectal area. Although some women enjoy anal stimulation, too, it seems to me that males have more capacity for pleasure here than females do. It is a wonderful opportunity for men to experience an internal orgasm similar to what some women feel vaginally. I used to feel sorry for men, thinking that they did not have as many erogenous zones as women do. Experience has taught me that men do have as many erogenous zones; sometimes they just need permission to enjoy them.

If my clients did not ask for anal stimulation, I often introduced the topic by asking them whether they were curious. Most would express fears that it might hurt, so I would recommend we just begin with light tickles of their anus. If they found that to be pleasurable—and most did—then I would ask them whether they wanted me to put my finger inside just a tiny bit. Curiosity usually won out over fear at this point. Some men loved the sensation, and some decided it was not for them. Those who found it pleasurable usually brought a variety of butt plugs to our next appointment. By the third appointment, we would most likely be shopping for a strap-on to suit his fancy.

So if you haven't experienced the male G-spot yet, and your partner's orgasms don't shake him up as much as a sneeze does, you might consider trying anal stimulation. It is not only erotic for the lucky male recipient, but in my opinion, it is very sexy fun for the female who is penetrating him.

23

Female Ejaculation and the Isis Squat

It would seem that we humans have a habit of forgetting what our forebears knew about sex. Consequently, we must discover sexual truths all over again. Over the years, there has been quite a bit of controversy regarding women's orgasms. First, it was asserted that vaginal orgasms were the only healthy orgasm for a woman to have while clitoral orgasms were an indication of childish and stunted sexual development. This preposterous stance on female sexual response was so severe in the minds of some medical professionals, that clitoridectomies were performed. In other words, to prevent women from experiencing sexual pleasure via the clitoris, the clitoris was surgically removed.

After women asserted their right to clitoral stimulation, we went the other way and declared that there was no such thing as a vaginal orgasm. All orgasms originated in the clitoris. Most experts now agree that most women experience clitoral orgasms, and at least some women can also experience vaginal orgasms. In fact, some women even experience orgasms resulting from stimulation of their cervix.

There also is the ongoing controversy regarding G-spots (short for Grafenberg) and female ejaculation. Is female ejaculate really a unique fluid, or is it just urine? Should women be allowed to enjoy ejaculating, or should they be considered incontinent and urged to seek treatment? Does the G-spot exist, or is it a myth? The only question I have is why do we expend so much energy analyzing and critiquing the way women get off? Isn't it more important that they experience pleasure, regardless of what part of their body is providing that pleasure?

For the record, some research has established the existence of female ejaculate. It has been analyzed and discovered to contain higher levels of glucose and an enzyme, prostatic acid phosphatase, characteristic of the prostatic component of semen. No one seems to agree on where this fluid comes from: some say the G-spot; some say the paraurethral glands; and some are sure it is the Skene's glands. Of course, some doctors are still calling it urine, and some research supports that assertion as well.

I don't think it matters much to your sex life where female ejaculate originates from nor what chemical components constitute it. If you are a female ejaculator, then you have another route to sexual pleasure and fulfillment. If you don't ejaculate, you may be able to teach yourself how to. Or you can leave well enough alone. The choice is yours.

I am a female ejaculator, and I can tell you that it provides me with an orgasm that is quite distinct from a vaginal orgasm. I don't stimulate my G-spot to ejaculate. I do have a G-spot, and I know exactly where it is, but I do not enjoy stimulating it. To ejaculate, I stimulate my clitoris. My ejaculate is usually oily to the touch and smells a little like walnuts. But sometimes some urine gets in there, too, and I know this because I can smell the ammonia. Who cares? Whether I ejaculate nothing but female ejaculate or a combination of ejaculate and urine, I feel wonderful! I just make sure I put a towel down so the sheets don't get wet and let nature take over.

My clitoral orgasms are more genitally focused, whereas my vaginal orgasms are total body orgasms that can take me to the point of being momentarily unconscious. On the other hand, my clitoral orgasms are incredibly intense, too. I have also combined clitoral and vaginal stimulation, adding anal stimulation, accentuating things by stimulating my nipples, using Tantric breathing to take sex someplace more spiritual, and so on.

The point is that there are many ways to find sexual bliss, and we don't need to form hierarchies in an attempt to determine which orgasms are the best. They are all good. Nor do we need to limit women's or men's sexual potential by invalidating their experience of their own bodies. Doctors and scientists read a lot of books and do some research, but that is not the same as actually having sex. I have had a lot of sex, and what I find to be true is "all of the above."

An important part of my training in sex included classes in Ancient Sacred Prostitution, which taught me to be proud of my female anatomy and imbued me with a more positive outlook on life, men, and sex. In particular, a technique called the Isis Squat helped to shift a paradigm for me. In my mind, it transformed my female genitals into a powerful muscle that would only become stronger with use.

These Ancient Sacred Prostitution classes were taught by Cosi Fabian in San Francisco, and she opened up a whole new reality for me. Ms. Fabian taught her students about the ancient prostitutes and transpersonal love. Her students were not necessarily prostitutes, and she wasn't teaching them how to be prostitutes. She taught something much deeper: Sex is a healing force, and women's genitals are sacred.

Ms. Fabian illustrated the Isis Squat, which involves the woman straddling the man's penis while he lies down. Instead of kneeling in the woman superior position, the woman stays firmly planted on her feet and uses her thigh muscles to propel herself up and down the penis. It gives the woman exquisite control over the rhythm, speed, depth, and direction of intercourse. It is easier for the woman to contract her PC muscles in this position. It also feels incredibly powerful.

When a woman straddles a man's penis on her knees, she cannot make the same deep and powerful strokes that she can if she is squatting on her feet. Women have strong thigh muscles, and it makes sense to use this part of our body to affect an assertive and powerful role during sexual intercourse. The man benefits as he gets to experience having sexual intercourse performed upon him. This is an extremely erotic experience for most men. I find the Isis Squat supremely satisfying on a multitude of levels, not the least of which is its orgasmic potential for the female.

Both women and men are capable of a variety of orgasmic responses. The orgasms can be different depending upon the type of stimulation, but they can also vary because of our ever-changing moods. Sometimes a particular body part is involved, and sometimes orgasms result from no physical contact whatsoever. Sexual response varies from person to person and from moment to moment. Our bodies are amazingly equipped to bring us pleasure and joy.

I recommend that if you have not already spent a fair amount of time getting to know your own anatomy and sexual response, that you do so. Nothing will improve partner sex to such a degree as masturbation. Masturbation is the most effective—and certainly the most enjoyable—way for you to learn how your body responds, what you like and what you don't like. After you are completely familiar with your sexuality, it will be much easier to communicate your desires and needs to your partner.

Your fingers are the best place to start. A mirror is helpful, too. By looking at your genitals, you will come to know them better and perhaps even learn to like the way they look. In my experience, having an appreciation for the appearance of my genitals has helped me to relax and enjoy sex more with a partner instead of wasting time feeling self-conscious.

Your fingers can give you immediate feedback regarding your sexual response because you can feel your clitoris become erect; you can feel your vagina lubricate; you can even feel your labia (inner and outer lips to your vagina) become engorged with blood and flatten and spread apart. Using your fingers, you can experiment by stimulating your clitoris with different degrees of pressure and speeds of movement. You can insert one or several fingers into your vagina and feel it come alive with movement. Practice squeezing your PC muscles while your fingers are inside of yourself so you get some idea of how powerful they are.

If you feel curious or desirous, you can move on to sex toys. You might enjoy experimenting with a few, such as a dildo, a vibrator, and perhaps a butt plug (see Chapter 22 for important tips on anal play). Maybe you will discover a favorite and decide to stick with it. Or you may enjoy the adventure of periodically trying something new. Give yourself permission to create pleasure in your life. It can only improve your outlook!

24

Lessons in Love for Him

A great deal of my time as an escort was engaged in educating men about the female body. Most of us have sex education during some portion of our educational process, but despite the diagrams and charts, we walk away knowing very little about how our bodies work. There really is no substitute for hands-on learning.

Presuming that you have familiarized yourself with your own anatomy, you can now teach what you know to your man. Get that hand mirror out so you can see what you are doing and invite your partner to join you this time. I usually use a reading lamp to illuminate my genitals for easy viewing. Although your approach will be more scholarly for this situation, there is no reason it cannot lead to sexual activity. Sometimes, the juxtaposition of cerebral and erotic stimuli is just what the doctor ordered!

In fact, many of my clients wanted just such an interaction when they were paying for my time. The first time I gave a man a hands-on lesson in female anatomy, I was sure the whole thing would be informative, but I doubted it could carry any sexual charge. As I matter-of-factly reclined on my massage table with my legs bent in the same position a woman assumes for a gynecological exam, sex was the last thing on my mind. I aimed a reading lamp right on my vulva so my student could get a good look while I explained in technical detail what he was looking at: "This is the clitoris, this is the vagina, this is the labia …."

To my surprise, he became very aroused. I had thought that I had to act sexy by being attentive to how I posed my naked body or what I said. I certainly did not think laying spread eagle on a massage table was going to be attractive. But I was wrong. Little did I know on that day that I would be doing repeat performances of this educational approach to foreplay for many years to come and always to rave reviews!

I have since come to the conclusion that the confidence it takes to be completely naked in daylight is sexy in and of itself. Add to that the assurance a woman must possess in order to spread her legs and direct a bright light onto her genitals, and you actually have created a very potent premise for arousal. But you are not finished with that. Now you are going to illustrate the ultimate in sexual courage and authority by 1) speaking about your genitals as if they were an interesting and worthy topic of conversation, and 2) requesting certain actions be performed specifically to please and pleasure you. What on earth could be sexier than that?

You can begin by asking your partner to touch the different parts of your genitals with you. Show him where your clitoris is and demonstrate the type of touch you prefer—directly on it, to the side, fast, slow, soft, or hard. Pull your labia majora open and make sure that he notices the labia minora inside if yours do not extend past your labia majora. Either way, be sure to point out to him that you have two sets of labia. I found that many men were unaware of this biological fact and quite entertained with its discovery.

Let him insert a finger into your vagina only if you actually will enjoy it. And be sure to tell him exactly how deep he should go, how many fingers he should use, whether you just want him to go in and stay there being very still or if you want him to move about after he's inside, and how you want him to move about if you do want him to move—back and forth, to the side, a wiggle or a stroke, and so on and at what speed. Don't forget to have him wear a latex glove if you are the least bit concerned about errant hangnails. Have some lube on hand in case you want extra lubrication, too.

Now the two of you can explore a part of your body that can be a little more difficult to access on your own. Although I know plenty of women who can find their G-spot with their own fingers just fine, it is not something that ever felt comfortable to me. I prefer that my partner does it. Even if you can find your G spot with ease, having your partner find it is an erotic moment you won't want to miss.

This is how you can teach him to stimulate your G-spot:

Make sure you are lying on your back with your knees slightly bent and have him insert his index finger about 1.5 to 2 inches into your vagina. He should do this with the palm of his hand facing up so that the tip of his finger can easily connect with the upper portion of your vagina (the side facing your stomach). When he is inside of you, have him make the "come here" motion with his index finger. With few minor adjustments, if any, he should contact a portion of your vagina that feels more sensitive to you. If he continues to rub this spot with his finger, it will get harder. That is because it contains erectile tissue similar to that found in a penis. This is the infamous G-spot.

If you are a female ejaculator, you may begin to feel like you are going to urinate at this point. If so, just relax and let nature take her course. You may expel ejaculate, urine, or some combination of the two. Don't worry what the liquid is, just let go and feel the waves of pleasure. If you are not a female ejaculator, you may still enjoy having your G-spot stimulated. Or you may not. Even if you are a female ejaculator, you may not enjoy the sensation of having your G-spot stimulated. I female ejaculate; I know right where my G-spot is; and I don't particularly enjoy having it stimulated with a finger or anything else for very long. A few seconds is all I care for, and I ejaculate from manipulating my clitoris. However, some women love stimulating their G-spots with fingers, dildos, a penis, and so on.

There is no right way or wrong way to get turned on. We are all individuals, and we should honor our individual sexual tastes. So don't worry about it. If you don't like how it feels, stop doing it (or have him stop). The point to this type of experimentation is twofold: 1) you learn more about your body and your sexual response, and 2) you are engaging in another form of foreplay with your partner, which can only lead to better sex one way or the other.

No doubt by now your man has become aroused, and he may be trying to move things along. Don't let him rush you past the cunnilingus lesson. If you have any feedback about his technique that you would like to share but may have been too embarrassed to tell him before, now is the time to do it. Few women agree on what constitutes perfect cunnilingus, and you should make sure that he knows this so he does not feel insecure or stupid. Assure him that if no two women are the same, he cannot be expected to know exactly how you like it. That's why you want to take this opportunity to share your preferences with him.

Don't just tell him what you like. Have him practice. In other words, you don't want to take his attention away from your genitals to look at your face while you talk to him. You want him to listen to you while he is attempting to duplicate your instructions. So ask him to go down on you and then give him gentle but clear feedback as he is doing it. "I like it a little harder." "Use more tongue and less lip." "It would feel even better if you put your finger inside of me while you tongue my clit." "Can you lick my anus, too?" These are examples of the straightforward instructions with which you can supply him. You don't have to say "please," and you don't have to put your sentences in the form of a question, although it is okay if you do.

Just keep in mind that simple, direct statements are the easiest to understand, and they help keep the focus on the action and off social dynamics. In the beginning I had a tendency to be a little hesitant or apologetic about asking for what I want in the way of sex. Even with clients who had requested sexual instructions, I found myself wasting time and energy trying to preface my feedback with praise. Eventually, I discovered it was unnecessary. Simple and direct instructions are the easiest to understand, and most men will welcome it! There is, however, one important caveat to this advice.

If the two of you decide to have intercourse after he has completed the cunnilingus lesson to your satisfaction, you should abandon some of the classroom affectation and allow yourself to slip into the passion of the moment. I have found that a little feedback during intercourse goes a long way. I prefer to give a man feedback about his style of sexual intercourse when we are not remotely interested in having sex with each other. I think this is a particularly sensitive subject for men, perhaps because so many men suffer from a greater or lesser degree of performance anxiety. It is better to have a separate conversation about the way you would like to have intercourse, rather than to pipe up during the act with a little constructive criticism. Otherwise, your sense of timing could elicit an undesirable effect: a failing erection.

Because you obviously want your feedback or constructive criticism to have the best possible chance of translating into better sex for both of you—be sure to use your intuition and gauge your lover's nonverbal cues while you are discussing your sexual desires with him. If he seems the least bit defensive, you may want to choose another time, setting, or approach. Stay focused on your objectives, but choose a delivery that will garner you the best results. Fortunately, you have his curiosity working in your favor, so your man probably won't require that much encouragement to pay attention to your comments—as long as he is cable of some multitasking: looking at and playing with your genitals while he listens to you give him feedback!

Again, humor is your best friend whenever you are introducing topics that can offend or threaten—and so is a certain amount of reassurance. We all need to feel safe and loved, and there is no time when this is more true than when someone who is very important to us is telling us how we can do better in bed. But be careful not to overdo it. No one likes to feel talked down to either. Insincere praise can sting more than a negative truth. Perhaps that is why I have had so much success with the classroom approach. It is neither judgmental nor patronizing. It just is.

25

Taking Control

I was shocked and amazed at how many of my clients craved being controlled in some manner. Because I had originally envisioned myself as getting paid to please, it never dawned on me that the majority of men longed for a woman to have power over them. If a man was extremely powerful in his day-to-day life and work, he wanted me to give him a complete break from that role. On the other hand, a man who felt dominated in life was not always so interested in being dominated in the bedroom, but there was still *some* interest in giving up sexual control.

Although I found a correlation between the jobs my clients held and the *degree* to which they wanted me to direct them and our sexual activities, the male desire for female dominance was extremely common. I concluded that regardless of a man's station in life, he had experienced sex as something that women either accepted or rejected from him. Most men tire of this leadership role in their relationships with women and need a break from it. So although there was a drastic difference in how mild or extreme the desire to be controlled was, it was nevertheless a rather universal desire among men.

The ways in which a woman can take control range from the seduction techniques I discussed in Chapter 13 to more emphatic forms of sex play, such as the use of restraints and even spanking. Some men wanted me to gently tie their wrists to the bedposts with my sheer stockings and then "have my way with them." Others longed to be handcuffed and blindfolded before I initiated oral sex. Some men wanted to be restrained and then denied sexual access to my body or their own. Despite protests to the contrary, many men love to be teased, taunted, and sexually frustrated. I know this is true, because they actually pay very good money for it.

This concept also came into play with the concept of body worship. Many men who wanted to adore the female form enjoyed being told how to please me. I would give them blunt criticisms about their style of lovemaking and insist that they perform perfectly for me. I would also insist that they keep their focus on my pleasure at all times and never let their hands stray to their own genitals.

Sexual desire can be fueled by sexual frustration. So allowing your man to see you naked (but delaying his ability to touch you) or initiating sexual intercourse (but warning him that he may not experience an orgasm until you say so) are ways to increase the orgasmic potential for both of you. This is a fairly simple truth you can illustrate for yourself when you masturbate. If you allow yourself to orgasm at the first possible moment, you will experience pleasure that is muted compared to the powerful orgasm(s) you can have if you masturbate longer. In a sense you are sexually frustrating yourself for a bigger payoff at the end. The same principle applies to partner sex.

As you experiment with control, you want to keep a few things in mind. First off, part of the appeal of this type of sex play can be the illusion that your partner is resisting. I remember getting terribly turned on as a college co-ed when I feigned indifference or a slight resistance to a would-be suitor's efforts to seduce me. I am not talking about a date rape situation in which you make it clear that you do not want to engage in sex and the guy decides that your "no" means "yes." I am speaking of mutual desire fueled by a little power play. Sometimes it is as innocent as a game of tag or tickle. One person is pursued while the other person resists.

Sex play is very much like any play, only instead of winning, you are playing for bigger and better orgasms and increased intimacy with your partner. While I encourage you to take the dominant role with your man and give him a break from having to initiate and orchestrate sex as well as bare the brunt of your occasional rejections (if in fact your relationship conforms to these typical gender roles), it is also fun to take the passive role and let him dominate you.

You can think about sex like a game of tag if it helps. First one chases, and then the other chases. "Tag, you're it!" Play usually involves switching places with your play partner at some point in the game, but not always. Some of us become quite attached to being the bad guy or the good guy in our play, and that's okay, too, as long as your partner's preferred role complements yours.

Simple forms of play can be a spontaneous activity, but many times when we are introducing someone to a new game, we take the time to discuss the rules. Especially when the rules to the game we want to play are complicated, we need to go over the details before we begin playing. Sex is no different. If you want to surprise your lover by loosely tying his ankles and wrists to the bed with a silk scarf before you practice your Isis Squat (see Chapter 23), you probably don't need to discuss this with him beforehand. Obviously, if he seems uncomfortable with this, you stop.

But if you are intent on introducing him to a pair of handcuffs and a blindfold, then you must talk to him first. You want to make sure that he finds the idea as erotic as you do. If you enjoy an element of surprise, you can discuss your desire ahead of time and let him know that you intend to spring this on him without further notice. As long as he shares your attraction to the element of surprise, you are good to go.

You never know what phobias or emergencies (muscle spasms, full bladder, migraine headache, and so on) might arise, and you need to know when to stop. Because part of the appeal is the illusion of resistance, you don't want him to simply tell you to "stop." Half the fun is when he acts like he doesn't want you to do this and tells you "no." *Safe words* are used instead of the words "no" or "stop." Some people use a color as a safe word. Red means "stop" in most street signs in most countries. Some people say "red" when they want the play to stop. Maybe you and your partner will find some other word that means something special to just the two of you. It only matters that you are both clear on what word you want to use to stop the action.

What if your partner doesn't like your idea for sex play? You can negotiate for something else. Find out what he doesn't like about your proposed scenario and see whether the two of you can create something that does work for him as well as you.

Maybe he has a thing about not being able to see, and he doesn't want to be blindfolded. Perhaps he would agree to a see-through scarf that looks like a blindfold but lets him see. Would this satisfy your fantasy of having him blindfolded? If so, you have a solution. If not, you keep negotiating. Maybe the blindfold is not so important to you. Maybe if he let you handcuff him to a chair that would make the situation more of a turn-on for you so you wouldn't even miss the blindfold.

The point, of course, is to discuss the things that appeal to you and the things that turn you off. Each of us is unique and so are our sexual fantasies and desires. There is no reason to be embarrassed about your feelings or judge the other person's feelings. This is an opportunity for the two of you to learn more about each other and yourselves. There is no right or wrong way to feel. And because you are already attracted to each other, chances are that you will be able to find compromises that work for both of you as long as you don't get defensive or attack your partner.

This is sometimes easier said than done. Growing up in a sex-negative world, most of us already feel defensive and judgmental about sex before we even begin the process of sharing and negotiating with our partners. So, most of your battles will be between your own ears. You have to feel comfortable with your own sexuality and fairly neutral on sexual topics before you can negotiate successfully for the sex you want. This is one of the special gifts I was able to give my clients—something all escorts give to their clients—an accepting and nonjudgmental space in which to be an authentic sexual being.

You can create an accepting and nonjudgmental space for your partner by first giving it to yourself. Resist the temptation to succumb to guilt and shame. Affirm sex as a natural, healthy, and very important aspect of life. Don't be afraid of your own fantasies, desires, and ecstasy. If you treat yourself with respect and dignity, it will become natural to extend that courtesy to others. And remember that as human beings we are neither better nor worse than each other, only different. It's a good thing that we are different; otherwise, life might be very boring. So celebrate your differences while you look for the common ground you can share, and you will be well on your way to creating new sexual frontiers to explore together!

26

Role Playing

As an escort, I spent a great deal of time role playing with my clients. Several men had such detailed fantasies that they actually presented me with written scripts! Their instructions, however, usually centered on what I was to wear and the words and actions to act out some sort of power dynamic.

Maybe I would be a desperate secretary pleading with her employer for a raise. Inevitably, I would resort to sex to convince my boss to see things my way. Or perhaps he had a female boss in real life, and his fantasy was that of her sexually harassing him and threatening to fire him if he did not give her a mind-blowing orgasm.

Some fantasies were obvious projections from real-life situations. Rather than risk the repercussions of acting on inappropriate fantasies, these men found a perfectly safe way to live out their fantasies. Other fantasies had little to do with the man's actual circumstances and might be something he saw in a movie or read in a book. His imagination had been sparked, and now he wanted to re-enact the scene that had aroused him.

Some men brought fantasies that I refused to indulge. I did not judge them as evil or wrong. I simply knew that I could not assist them with their fantasy role play because it pushed too many of my buttons. I found myself angered or frightened by their fantasies, and so I had no business facilitating those fantasies for them.

You may find some of your partner's fantasies insulting or revolting. You should not engage in fantasy play that makes you uneasy. For example, you should never let anyone tie you up or otherwise gain control over you unless you trust them implicitly. As an escort, I never indulged a client fantasy if it involved putting me in a compromised position. As long as you take that precaution, you can feel free to explore the erotic potential of your mind. It is, after all, the biggest sex organ humans have.

You and your partner can share plenty of fantasies without either of you doing anything that makes you feel uncomfortable. One way to do this is by being specific about the rules of your role playing before you actually begin. I want to reiterate the fact that having a safe word is very important. For instance, if your partner's fantasy includes saying "no," you don't want to confuse a real "no" with a pretend "no," so having another word (for instance the color "red") can remove that potential for confusion in the heat of passion. And by all means, after you have agreed to the rules, play by them without exception. If you don't, you run the risk of violating your partner's trust, and he may not want to play with you again.

In the spirit of having fun, it doesn't hurt to try a few fantasies that may at first seem silly or less than sexy to you. You may be surprised to find that after you get into role playing, you actually enjoy yourself more than you expected. For example, some men tend to have fantasies involving varying degrees of forcible or restrained sex.

This was a typical scenario that I was asked to enact many times. It involved pushing the man down onto the bed and then roughly tying his hands and feet to the bedpost. I would always let him decide whether I would use nylon stockings, rope, or handcuffs. This was one way I could gauge how extreme his fantasy was if he had been less than forthcoming. I found a lot of men who harbored a rape fantasy were at least mildly embarrassed about it and couldn't always speak about it in detail. Instead, they would whisper "I want you to make me give you pleasure."

So if he chose nylon stockings, I knew he was looking for a rape fantasy that was more gentle and romantic. I would maintain a more playful attitude while still performing the same actions. Rope meant he was more serious about the fantasy and wanted me to act at least a little mean or demanding. And if he selected handcuffs, he was probably ready for a fantasy that was as near to reality as fantasy can get. Again, in all three cases my actions would be very similar, but my attitude and my energy would vary. I found that attitude and energy are really the key ingredients to any fantasy role playing. It can be playful or humorous, or it can be very serious.

It just depends upon what turns you and your partner on and even that can vary from day to day, so it is a good idea to make sure that you understand what kind of mood your partner is in and that the two of you are on the same energy level. You want your fantasy role playing to be a total turn-on for both of you and something that you will both want to do again and again. So it is important to avoid assumptions and get some clarification as to your partner's desires in the moment. What worked last week may not fit for today.

In addition to the type of fantasy you are enacting, the words you use have a great deal of power. For example, there is a big difference between "you've been a naughty boy" and "shut up, slave." The former tends to be a bit playful, and the other is full-on fantasy role playing—more like acting than play acting. Some people also love to talk dirty and to be talked dirty to. Some people find that extremely offensive and a complete turn-off. Obviously, it helps to know your partner's preferences in this department. But I also found that I could gauge this pretty well simply by paying attention to my partner's facial expressions, body language, and breathing. His erection was also a fairly good indicator, although not a foolproof one.

So after immobilizing a man with the restraint of his choice, I would usually play with his nipples and penis just enough to torture him with the teasing. Then I would stand over him so he could see my vulva before I actually sat upon his face and demanded that he perform cunnilingus. After he had completed this task to my satisfaction, I would ensure that his penis was as hard as I wanted it to be by either using my hands or my mouth to further stimulate him, and then I would hop onto his penis using the Isis Squat (see Chapter 23 for details of this little known but amazing sexual position).

Most men were so turned-on at this point that they would experience an orgasm almost immediately. Perhaps not such a good thing if you want him to last longer for your sake. But if you don't want him to ejaculate at all, you can prevent it simply by stopping the movement while he is inside of you or getting off his penis entirely. Of course, because this was the man's rape fantasy, my focus was on fulfilling his fantasy by giving him the ultimate orgasm as soon as he felt the urge! Presumably, I had already had an orgasm while he was being "forced" to give me pleasure.

The number and diversity of role plays you and your partner can engage in are limited only by your imagination. Some people enjoy dressing up in costumes just like they did as children. You can pretend to be a naughty nurse or a deviant doctor. You might want your man to wear a G-string under his clothes and strip for you. Some women take belly dancing lessons so they can dance privately for their man. You can try scripting a very complicated scene complete with dialog just as if you were making a movie. But whether you use fancy props or only the dynamics of the role play, the point is to have fun and explore yet another way to increase your potential for erotic joy.

27

Exhibitionism as an Aphrodisiac

If you find that dressing up in sexy lingerie is a turn-on for you, you might also like to try letting your partner take photos of you in your lingerie or even while you are naked. And if that appeals to you, you might also enjoy getting out your camcorder for some really advanced exhibitionism!

I understand that many women will feel compelled to draw the line at making home movies. Some may feel too self-conscious about their bodies or how they might look while having sex. Others might be morally against the whole concept. Maybe they think having their lovemaking on film will somehow cheapen it. Certainly, we are all entitled to our opinions, and if you feel strongly about anything, you have the right to assert powerful boundaries for yourself. Never do anything that you do not want to do, especially when it comes to sex. But if you are on the fence on the topic—a bit intrigued but perhaps timid about it—this chapter will offer some tips that will help you to experiment and have fun finding out whether it is for you.

The first time I saw myself naked on video I was relieved. The physical defects I imagined myself to possess were not as extreme in reality. My self-concept simply did not reflect the facts. I looked sexier than I thought I would. That doesn't mean I was perfectly happy with everything I saw. I had a couple small rolls of fat on my tummy that I resolved to get rid of. But the overall effect of seeing myself having sex was that it boosted my self-esteem and increased my ability to enjoy sex. I was able to let go of some of my self-consciousness and start enjoying sex more.

I also discovered that I love everything about making my own porn. For me, being in front of the camera while having sex is a powerful turn-on. I have had some of my very best orgasms while the camera was running. And I get to recapture the sexual heat of the moment when I made the pornographic video by watching it after it is made. This is something I don't do alone, although you certainly could. I just prefer to watch my porn with my partner. Again, it is the act of being an exhibitionist that is the turn-on for me. Watching my partner watch me is what turns me on after I have made a video.

I should probably note here that if you do find that exhibitionism is part of your sexual landscape, just as with other forms of sexual expression, exhibitionism must be consensual. Exhibiting yourself to unsuspecting strangers is against the law and may lead to your incarceration. If you want to explore exhibitionism, make sure that your intended audience has given their consent.

As you experiment with exhibitionism, I recommend that you begin with lingerie. As little girls, most of us played dress-up, and dressing up in lingerie is not that different. Of course, now you don't have to pretend to have a woman's body. You do. And you don't have to worry about being too sexual or too obvious. In fact, the more sexual and obvious you feel like being, the better!

You should begin in private in front of a full-length mirror. This will give you a chance to figure out which lingerie you think looks best on you. You can also practice some sexy poses in front of the mirror—remember doing that as a little girl? Have fun, whatever you do. Come to appreciate your womanly attributes, and it will carry over into the way you walk, talk, and hold yourself.

After you feel comfortable in private, you are ready to make your entrance. Tell your man you want a date for some hot sex! Tell him to prepare the room with candles and music while you change into something more comfortable. Be prepared for his jaw to drop when you walk into the room. No matter how many times he has seen you naked, most men will respond to lingerie as if they are seeing you for the first time. Now keep in mind that there is this small percentage of men who don't care for lingerie. If your man is one of these rare birds, then you can invite him to undress you as quickly as possible! Regardless of his proclivity for lingerie, he will know that you went to the extra trouble to present yourself in a special way for him. And the lingerie may have the effect of boosting your body confidence. Those two factors can increase the sexual heat between you as well.

I wore so much lingerie while escorting that I felt completely comfortable in it. However, I do remember one occasion when a particular client made an unusual request regarding lingerie. He asked me to dine in his hotel room wearing only a push-up bra, garters, stockings, and classic pumps. He wore his military uniform. So while he sat there fully dressed, I proceeded to eat and engage in conversation wearing nothing but lingerie. I must admit it created a great deal of sexual tension. I think the fact that one of us was completely dressed and the other was almost naked, combined with the fact that we were engaging in activities people usually wear clothes for—eating and talking about current affairs—created the erotic heat. Maybe you would like to try something similar with your guy!

A lot of men actually love to go shopping for lingerie for the women in their lives. Of course, some men are too embarrassed to do so. But if your man is in the former category, you may find this is another way to add spice to your love life. I have been literally showered with lingerie and accessories over the years: bra and panty ensembles, garters and stockings, lacy teddies, colored and/or textured pantyhose, leather bikinis, thigh-high boots, classic red pumps, bodysuits, satin gloves, sexy little t-shirts, and latex corsets!

One gentleman stood out in particular. He never showed up empty-handed. Every time I saw him he brought me clothes: lingerie, shoes, dresses, skirts, blouses, scarves, and so on. He loved the entire process—fantasizing about me in a particular ensemble, shopping for the items that fit his fantasy, giving those clothes as a gift, and then watching me try each outfit on for him. I would take the clothes into my walk-in closet, change, and then make my grand entrance just for his viewing pleasure. As I walked around the room modeling my new clothing, he would eye my every curve with a sense of satisfaction. Then, before returning to my closet to change into the next outfit, I would tease him by sitting on his lap and letting him rub his hands all over me through the fabric.

By the time I was modeling the second or third ensemble, I switched tactics and performed a striptease for him. I wore sexy lingerie under a dress or maybe a short skirt with a sheer blouse so he could get a hint of what was underneath. First, I unbuttoned the blouse slowly and seductively, or I invited him to unzip my dress—careful not to allow him to make any other contact with my body. I strutted around the room with confidence while I proceeded to reveal a bra strap on one shoulder. My fingers found their way under my bra and to my own nipple. I gave it a squeeze while I closed my eyes in reverie.

Then I turned my back on him and slowly let the dress or the blouse fall to the floor. If I was still wearing a skirt, I unzipped it myself while my back was still facing him and then let that fall to the floor as well. Bending over ever so slightly, I rubbed my own posterior with both of my hands and gave a playful slap to one cheek. As I turned around, I shot him a seductive and arrogant glance and then brought my attention back to myself. My hand found its way under my thong and onto my clitoris. I let myself surrender to the pleasurable feelings for only a moment, and then I continued to disrobe.

I turned my back to him once again while I unhooked my bra and let it fall to the floor. Facing him again, I fondled both of my own breasts and then began pulling at my thong. First I pulled it up into myself so that my labia were exposed; then I pulled it to one side so he could see my vulva. As I pulled the thong from side to side, it aroused me more. Then I slipped out of the thong and was standing there in nothing but thigh highs and heels! I need not tell you what happened next. But if you aren't sure what happens next, I suggest you give a similar performance for your man!

If your partner is excited about seeing you in lingerie, you might also invite him to take some photos of you. You can use a Polaroid or digital camera to eliminate the need for film and preserve your privacy. Many digital cameras allow you to take still photos as well as short videos. Experiment with both if you have the opportunity. Let yourself go and flaunt your best assets. This is the time to be naughty and free from the inhibitions of your day–to-day life. You can show off your legs, cleavage, and posterior. If you are feeling really brave, you can even show a little "pink" by pulling your panties or G-string off to the side and exposing your vulva.

Some couples will keep the camera focused on the female, and others will want to take turns taking erotic photos of each other. If your man is open to the idea, you may find that being behind the camera is also erotic for you. It can be a lot of fun to direct your man while he plays at being your own private model. You can tell him to take off his shirt and play with his nipples. Then have him remove his shorts and stroke himself while you take photos of his growing erection.

After the two of you have experimented with lingerie and erotic images of each other, you may want to try something more advanced. Have you ever wondered what you look like while you are having sex? Well, now is the time to find out!

Filming yourself while you are having sex takes a little bit of expertise. I am sure you have seen plenty of home videos of anniversaries and family reunions where the lighting is so terrible that everyone's faces are washed out? Well, that can happen with a sexual home movie as well, only the bad lighting will be reflected in the way your skin looks all over your body!

I recommend you experiment first without actually having sex. Run some video footage just to get an idea of your background and lighting as well as how your skin looks under these conditions. If your camera is sophisticated, you can no doubt program it to make the proper compensations. Otherwise, you might need to invest in a little lighting equipment. Keep in mind that professional lighting is what makes or breaks careers in film, television, and modeling. It is a science that requires an extensive education as well as years of experience to be truly proficient.

Don't expect your results to look professional. Part of the charm of amateur adult videos is the bad lighting and sound. But you want to make sure that your results are not so unprofessional that you can't enjoy watching it. If you experiment with these technical aspects of making videos before you actually have sex on camera, you won't be left wondering whether the video looks bad because you are the ones having sex in it. This is a common fear, and you can get past that by being familiar with your video equipment as well as the amateur porn that other couples make.

After you know what the limitations of your video equipment and location are, then you can adjust your expectations for the actual video. This will help you to interpret your results in context. Instead of expecting your video to look like a major motion picture, you will know that you can expect it to look only as good as your camera and lighting will allow.

It can be very helpful to view the amateur porn other couples have made. Some couples enjoy taking their home movies and/or photos out of their bedroom and sharing them on the Internet. If you want to check out some completely noncommercial home-produced porn, visit the personal web pages of couples listed on Jane's Guide (www.janesguide.com). You can also find plenty of amateur porn on the Internet, but be careful that you don't buy the professionally produced porn that is labeled "amateur."

When amateur porn hit the market, it was an overnight sensation because couples wanted to see other couples having real sex—not actors faking sex. Unfortunately, many mainstream production companies have tried to capitalize on the amateur market by labeling the fake stuff they produce as amateur. But there is no mistaking the two art forms. One is real, and the other is obviously acted. If you want to be completely safe, search for the free amateur porn on the Internet. This will lead you to home movies made by couples just like you. They just happen to enjoy taking their exhibitionism onto the Internet. Who knows, you may get some ideas for making your own erotic photos or movies.

Another important consideration for home movies is the position of the camera in relation to what it is filming. You will want to experiment with the tripod and your zoom to make sure that your camera is in the best possible position to capture all the action and that you have framed it properly. Some angles are less flattering than others, so experiment until you find what works best. After you have a handle on these technical aspects to home movies, you can start having fun.

My husband and I had the opportunity to be filmed having sex for The Playboy Channel. The entire film was only about 10 minutes long when it aired. However, the interview process lasted about two and a half days! One bedroom scene took an entire day to shoot because they spent hours adjusting the lighting. By the time they got done, it looked as if the moon was shining into our bedroom and reflecting romantically off the ceiling (there was no moonlight—they had installed lights outside the window and used filters to project that light onto the ceiling). The candlelight cast a romantic mood. The soft focus lens created a dreamy state of mind. Everything was perfect, and it showed in the end result.

You cannot expect your photos or your videos to look as if they have had the hours of professional lighting and expertise that professional photos and films employ. So get a feel for what is possible with your photography and video equipment and then have fun!

Depending upon how much difficulty you have experienced in getting the technical aspects where you want them, you may need to videotape yourself on another day. In some ways this may be a blessing as it will give you more time to warm up to the idea. I find that problem solving can alleviate a case of the nerves quite nicely. When you are ready to take that leap in front of the camera, you want to be able to get out of your head and into the sexual heat. This is one reason I insist that you get the technical aspects figured out up front, because nothing is more disappointing than feeling hot and sexy but seeing little of that captured in your movie!

Ideally, you will have the camera, lights, and background arranged to your satisfaction so that all you need do is turn the camera on and step in front of it. You may choose to shoot short sections of your lovemaking so you can stop and watch yourselves. Each time you stop to watch, you will hopefully find yourself becoming more aroused so that the next scene will be even hotter. Of course, if you prefer to ignore the camera and make love straight through, you can always watch it later as a way of generating sexual heat for another sexual interlude.

As you experiment, remain open to your ever-changing perceptions and feelings. The only way you can truly learn what you like is by trying new things with an open mind. But be clear on the fact that we are all individuals and what works for some does not work for all. Giving yourself permission to experiment is only safe if you know how to walk away from a failed experiment. If you find that anything suggested in this book is not for you, then simply chalk it up as more valuable information and move on to the next chapter.

So what are you waiting for? Buy yourself some brand new sexy lingerie (you deserve it) and see what develops next!

28

When Your Man Needs a Little Extra Help

Erectile Dysfunction (ED) has come out of the closet and into our homes via Viagra commercials. What was once whispered about, if acknowledged at all, is now fodder for family humor. But impotence is no laughing matter for the man who suffers from it or for his sexual partner. It is estimated that as many as 30 million men suffer from impotence in the United States alone. Therefore, the chances that you may have to deal with it on a personal level at some time in your life are rather high.

During my career as an escort, I encountered male impotence on a regular basis. In fact, I am convinced that this is one of the major reasons many men go to see escorts. They are often hoping that a professional will know how to get them past their impotence. Clients hope the escort will know a special trick that will restore them to their old sexual selves. Of course, it is never as easy as that. Many factors can create erectile dysfunction in a man. And figuring out which combination of factors is influencing an individual man's sexual performance is not a straightforward task. A multitude of emotional, psychological, and physical elements can contribute to impotence in any given man.

Many men also endure occasional bouts of impotence without it being a major influence on their sex lives. It is a rather common occurrence for men of all ages to experience some fluctuations in the dependability of their erection. Unfortunately, some poor souls focus on that one less-than-impressive incident and in so doing precipitate even more episodes. It becomes a self-fulfilling prophecy of sorts. The more the man obsesses over the one time he could not achieve an erection, the more likely he is to suffer erectile difficulties in the future. Anxiety does nothing good to the blood flow needed to sustain an erection. The more anxious a man is, the less likely his penis is to become erect. So the number one word of advice for men with any level of erectile dysfunction is RELAX!

I often used humor to coax a client into relaxing enough to allow his penis to achieve an erection. I would make him focus on my sexual pleasure while I was in charge of his. If at any time, he tried to make his penis his business, I would tell him "naughty boy" and "that is none of your business — you leave that to me." It was actually great fun to show a man how much "normal" function his penis was capable of in the right hands.

But not all men experience erection difficulties due to a case of the nerves. Presuming his problems are not purely self-created due to his emotions, many men will require medical help in order to resume a satisfying sex life. Impotence can be caused by physical, emotional, and psychological factors. Depression, stress, anxiety, exhaustion, illness, and injury can have devastating effects on the libido and sexual function.

As an escort, I most often encountered impotence resulting from alcohol abuse, smoking, and performance anxiety. The tragedy is that all of these are self-inflicted. A healthy lifestyle devoid of addictions is the first line of defense against impotence. If someone is addicted to alcohol, cigarettes, or other chemicals, there is nothing you can do about it. They have to want to change and that doesn't usually happen until something serious wakes them up to the price they are paying.

Many of the men I saw were under the false impression that their penis had stopped working properly. They would complain that they could not achieve or sustain an erection. I always asked them whether they were still masturbating (it eliminates the impulse to deny this private pleasure if you just assume it happens). The answer was usually "yes" and then I would ask whether they were able to stay hard until they ejaculated while masturbating. If they said "yes," I would point out that their penis was obviously functioning just fine. Then we could turn our attention to the circumstances that might induce an otherwise healthy penis to become timid.

Of course, many men actually have a combination of physical and psychological factors impacting their abilities to achieve and sustain an erection. I always approach the possible emotional and psychological issues first, because even if the problem turns out to be mostly physical, most men have developed a plethora of negative feelings about themselves and sex as a result. Humans must be treated as a whole organism and not a collection of body parts, and nowhere is that more important than when it comes to sexuality.

A lot of men lose their erection at the moment of penetration, which is more of a psychologically induced condition. I would encourage them to first acknowledge the timing of their lost erection and then to consider possible reasons for it. I always kept things on the light side and encouraged laughter on their part. Sometimes I would speak to them on behalf of their penises, encouraging them to see things from "his" point of view. Maybe a new partner's genitals were frightening the life right out of "him." Or perhaps the expectation that "he" should stay hard and not ejaculate until his partner was totally satisfied had become a laborious and joyless task instead of an event to anticipate with enthusiasm.

I did not assign blame, but I did interject humor. I found this approach enabled many men to reconnect with the pleasurable and carefree aspects of lovemaking. I was careful to keep the focus on sexual pleasures other than intercourse and off the concept of performing. In my opinion, both men and women would benefit immeasurably by rejecting any type of thinking that envisions sex as something that needs to be performed or done correctly. The competitive nature of our society has invaded our bedrooms, and for many people, this has led to anxiety-induced sexual dysfunction.

Hopefully, either because you have read this book or because you already knew this to be true, you have an enlarged view of what sex is so that even if your man experiences some erectile dysfunction, the two of you can turn to sexual delights other than intercourse and sustain your connection and intimacy. Given the best of circumstances, sex is rarely the same every time we do it. Sometimes it is more exciting than others. Sometimes the orgasms are huge and mind-blowing, and other times they are adequate. Try not to get fixated on a particular sexual result and learn to enjoy the process or path you take to sexual connection. As they say, "getting there" is half the fun!

That said, you can use some specific techniques to assist an erection in some circumstances. I have experienced varying results with different men, and those results have been primarily contingent on the man's overall health. For example, I have had no luck circumventing the circulatory problems that diabetes poses. It is a powerful disease, and it wreaks havoc with men's erections. If your man has diabetes, you will need to seek help from his doctor to restore his ability to achieve an erection. I did have one diabetic client who was able to sustain rock-hard erections. He used a pump he had prescribed to him by his doctor. The results would have made a teenage boy blush!

I also haven't had much luck getting past the circulatory problems that alcohol can pose. Especially in men who are in advanced stages of alcoholism, erections can be almost nonexistent. Again, if your man has a problem with alcohol, you have "bigger fish to fry" as they say. Get him some help if he will cooperate.

But let's say your man has neither of these major illnesses to contend with, and he is experiencing erectile dysfunction just the same. You might begin with humor as previously stated. Also focus on taking the slightest hint of performance anxiety out of the equation. You can do this by insisting that he pleasure you with his hands and tongue. You can try commanding him not to get hard (reverse psychology doesn't just work on children; it can also work on a man's penis). Then tell him to put himself in your capable hands and take the day off.

You can begin by taking the base of his penis in one hand while gently stroking the glans of his penis with your other hand. Put it in your mouth, too, but don't take your hand off the base of his penis. Basically you are going to use that hand like a cock ring (a small ring of rubber or other material that is placed at the base of a flaccid penis). This ring holds the blood in the penis, causing an erection to become more pronounced. You can achieve a similar result with your hand, and the reason I prefer working with my hand is because it helps to reduce performance anxiety. I have seen too many men with erectile problems resort to cock rings only to be disappointed. Treating the blood flow problem without working on the man's mind and emotions has not produced very impressive results in my experience. Even if I wanted to use a cock ring, I would begin with my warm, friendly hand.

While keeping the blood in the penis with one hand, I usually use my other hand and my mouth to provide a variety of stimulation simultaneously. So while I am holding the base of his penis with my hand and sucking the head of his penis with my mouth, I will use my free hand to stroke the shaft of his penis, stimulate his testicles, touch his perineum, and/or penetrate his rectum with my finger. I don't forget to stimulate his nipples, either.

The effect is to provide so much stimulation that he has to stop thinking and worrying at some point and simply surrender to the sensations. This works for some men. For others, this is too much stimulation to concentrate on getting hard or having an orgasm. So for these individuals I recommend slowly alternating with the stimulation you provide with that spare hand until you notice which form of stimulation is providing the most arousal. Then stick with that third form of sexual arousal and perfect your pressure and pace. Again pay attention to what seems to increase blood flow to his penis. Is it slow and gentle stimulation or strong and fast?

The end result will still involve both of your hands and your mouth. But instead of alternating between erogenous zones, you will stick to just three: the glans of his penis, the base of his penis, and one other spot that really turns him on. Just think of all the fun you will have discovering what that third mystery spot is.

Please don't be disappointed if these techniques do not garner the desired result. Not only do I refuse to play into the performance anxiety of others, I don't subject myself to the whip of performance anxiety. Even when men were paying me good money to "make" them experience an orgasm, I did not lose any sleep if I was unable to do so. First, I always kept in mind that there might be underlying health issues of which I was not aware. Second, I reminded myself that I cannot really give anyone an erection or an orgasm, I can only make it more likely. Each of us is responsible for our own sexual response and fulfillment. And finally, sex is more than erections and orgasms, and it is my job to make sure that everyone with whom I work remembers that.

Although the most talked-about form of sexual impotence is in regard to men, women also can suffer from sexual impotence. Some women find that Viagra can assist them in the same way it does men by increasing blood flow to their genitals for increased arousal. However, be advised that although some doctors are now prescribing Viagra for women, it has not been approved by the FDA for this purpose. Testosterone patches and creams have also proved successful in restoring sexual desire and response in women. But again, the testosterone patches are not FDA-approved at this time. Apparently improving women's sex drive is not yet a priority with the people in charge of making these decisions.

Many couples have renewed their enthusiasm for each other and life in general by seeking assistance for impotence and/or a lagging libido as a team. It certainly helps to take the onus off of either partner who might otherwise feel to blame. For this reason, I highly recommend therapy or couples counseling if you even suspect there may be any psychological or emotional factors that need to be addressed in your relationship. I can't begin to tell you what a boon to my sex life couple's counseling proved to be for me.

Some sexual difficulties are due to health conditions that are considered handicaps. I prefer the term "differently-abled." Many people assume that people in wheelchairs or with major malformations of their bodies are no longer sexual beings. This is completely false. I have had sex with men who are quadriplegic (paralyzed in both their arms and legs); men with colostomy bags (a bag worn on the outside of the body where the contents of the bowels are collected); men missing a leg, an arm, or both hands; men in wheelchairs; and even a thalidomide survivor.

A thalidomide survivor is someone born with birth defects because their mother took thalidomide during her pregnancy. Defects are numerous and varied but often include severe deformity of the limbs including the substitution of flippers for arms and/or legs. The man who came to see me wore both arm and leg braces because he had only flippers where these limbs should have been. He bounded into my room with the biggest blue eyes I have ever seen and a bright smile to match. He proceeded to remove his braces and climb onto my bed. I was suddenly face to face with a head and a torso. Having worked with a variety of disabilities, I was a little shocked at how ill at ease I felt. I expected more from myself. Either he didn't notice, or he was used to working past people's fears. While he gazed deep into my eyes, he stroked my neck and shoulders with the appendage located where an arm might have been. I was surprised to feel my body shudder with sexual pleasure at his touch. Soon I forgot all about my fear, and I could see him for the whole sexual being that he was. I will never forget this man. He may very well be one of the sweetest and happiest men I will ever meet.

Some people think sex should be reserved for those persons who are healthy, young, and whole. But sex is for everyone. Sex is a very important aspect of being alive, and to deny the sexuality of people who are differently-abled or aged is to deny them the dignity of being fully human. In fact, those stubborn individuals who have insisted upon maintaining a healthy sex life no matter whether they conform to societal standards for sex appeal or not, reap a multitude of benefits in addition to the pleasure and intimacy associated with sexual activity.

The benefits of sex include better cholesterol levels, increased circulation, improved immunity, decreased risk of developing prostate problems in men, stronger bones and muscles, more endorphins (which means less pain), stress reduction, a slowing of the aging process, and a general sense of well-being. Why would anyone want to deny this kind of healing for differently-abled persons, or any other consenting adult for that matter?

Depending upon the specific condition, certain adjustments do have to be made to facilitate sex for the differently-abled. For instance, quadriplegics rarely experience any physical sensation in their genitals, but they can learn to experience sexual arousal and even orgasm using different parts of their body, such as their necks and ear lobes. You already know that it is possible for us to experience orgasm independent of our genitals. (Remember Tantric sex in Chapter 21?) If you or your partner are quadriplegic, I highly recommend you study Tantra. Who knows, after you have learned to stimulate yourself and your partner through Tantric breathing, you may discover that sex is even better than it was before your condition!

One of my former clients is quadriplegic. I came to visit him off and on for more than 10 years. He taught me so much about the persistence of sexuality in the face of major obstacles. And he opened my eyes to the beauty that is sex, no matter what body we may have. Since he is paralyzed in both his arms and legs, he has little sexual sensation in his genitals. But he has a very full sex life. He has channeled his sexuality into a more spiritual realm, incorporating Tantric breathing and some role playing and other sex play that does not require an erect penis. Oh, and did I mention he loves to perform cunnilingus?

The important thing to remember is that most of the difficulty we experience with sex really begins in our minds. Often we have a limited definition of sex that reduces our abilities to experience pleasure and joy. And because we put undue pressure on ourselves and/or our partners to look a certain way or perform a certain way, we end up removing the most essential aspect to sex—the act of letting go! You can't let go if you are preoccupied with feelings of low self-worth. You can't let go if you are attempting to control your partner. And you can't let go if your head is full of thoughts about how you should look, how long you should last, or how or when you should have an orgasm.

Even in instances where a physical condition restricts or alters your sexual function, so many sexual options are still available that you need never experience anything less than a satisfying and fulfilling sex life. But you will have to expand your awareness of sexual alternatives. If you insist on keeping sex narrowly defined as a penis inside a vagina, you will no doubt cheat yourself out of untold happiness even if you can accomplish the act. That mindset is simply too restricted to even allow all that is possible during intercourse. Sex is so much bigger than our bodies. Sex begins and ends in our brains and hopefully in our hearts. If you expand your definition of sex to embrace sensual love and spiritual intimacy, your body may surprise you with what it is capable of.

As an escort, even when my ultimate aim was sexual intercourse, I took my sweet time getting there, and I did my best to distract my partner so he would not be single-mindedly focused on a goal. Goals are fine for the office and sports. But in the bedroom, stop thinking about your destination and start enjoying the sights along the way! Touching and kissing, hugging and holding, laughing and crying ... these are elements of human interaction, which have an important place in our sexual relating. If we comprehend what a gift it is to be that close to another human being and to share that level of intimacy, then sexual function does not necessarily deserve the spotlight. Although I value orgasms as much as the next person, I know only too well that chasing them will usually cause them to run away.

29

Sex and Spirit

In my own search for ever better sex, I have realized that sex is extremely fulfilling for me when it embodies a spiritual component. Some people become confused and even frightened if sex is referred to as being "spiritual." But there is nothing to be afraid of. In fact, you probably already experience a spiritual component to your sex life. You just may not be fully aware of it, and, if you are like most people, you probably perceive some separation between sex and the spiritual side of life.

My personal journey to heal this artificial separation between my sexual self and my spiritual self began by studying ancient goddess cultures. Before exposing myself to this part of history, I had no idea that sex was ever considered anything but an embarrassing fact or a necessary evil. I learned of a time when sex was seen as a joyful and pleasurable union—a celebration of life! Sex was also revered because it could lead to the creation of another life. Sex was holy, not profane. It was not that our forebears attempted to remove sex from the physical plane and impose grandiose spiritual attributions to justify it. Rather, they did not perceive a contradiction between the body's fleshy reality and the mind's aspirations for spiritual fulfillment.

I find it helpful to know that today's reality was not always the only reality. Putting current cultural norms and expectations into a historical context can be quite freeing if for no other reason than when someone tells you "that's the way it has always been" you know they are wrong. Some things have been with us for a very long time, but if you go back far enough in human history, which is after all a very short span of time, you can find cultural norms that contradict those we hold dear today. This can have the effect of giving you permission to establish your own standards rather than submitting to the expectations of others.

In my pursuit of more spiritual sexual expression, I have encountered some individuals who feel a need to establish hierarchies. So rather than just enjoy the merits of Tantric or Sacred Sex, they bring a belief that these forms of sex are morally superior to other forms of sex. I do not ascribe to any such worldview. I prefer to embrace the variety of sexual expressions, not only for others, but also for myself. I enjoy having sex on a purely physical plane, and I am in awe of the spiritual side of sex. I choose to celebrate this diversity of sexual truth. Besides, it seems to me that adhering to moral hierarchies falls severely short of spiritual aspirations. Hierarchies are another way that we judge others and attempt to assert our egos by pretending to superiority. Humility cannot live in such an environment. And humility is necessary if we are to be teachable. Ideally, life should be a journey of learning. Sex is no different.

The sexual shame that permeates our culture today began with this "my sex is better than your sex" attitude. For many years the missionary position (male superior intercourse position) was touted as morally superior to other forms of heterosexual intercourse. With the Sexual Revolution (the 1960s "free love" movement), such attitudes were supposedly revealed as sexist and limiting propaganda. But in its place some erected new sexual ideals with which to intimidate others. For instance, some women felt pressured to submit to sex even if they didn't desire it for fear of being seen as square or frigid. Then in the '70s the New Age Movement (spiritual movement also referred to as metaphysical that embraces meditation, affirmations, astrology, and so on) revived ancient sexual practices such as Tantra, and once again some were tempted to assert that "my sex is better than your sex."

I would prefer to learn all these different ways of having sex and incorporate each to greater and lesser degrees into my personal sex life. Only you can decide what meets your needs and desires best, and you may change your mind from time to time, too. Good for you if you do! The more sexual experience you accumulate (even in a relationship with one partner), the happier you are likely to be. At the very least, you will succeed in getting to know yourself better. And your sex life should be about you—not impressing some imaginary audience.

During my 14 years as an escort I discovered that my clients, for whatever reason, were more prone to worship women than objectify them. In the beginning, I attracted plenty of men who objectified me, but as my career progressed, these superficial souls disappeared, and I only shared time with substantial individuals who longed to service the Goddess incarnate. They probably would not choose those words, but nevertheless their actions expressed this sentiment.

I have been showered with love, gifts, and money. But what has touched me most deeply has been the degree of vulnerability with which my clients have trusted me. Whether grieving the death of a family member, dealing with a physical disability or disfigurement, struggling with major life decisions or facing their own mortality, I have been honored to share the most private of thoughts and emotions. And that has lent a depth of fulfillment to my career in the sex industry for which I never ever hoped.

Because of the nature of sex work, I was allowed to peer deep into the naked and vulnerable side of men. I went from having a certain amount of animosity toward men in general to feeling compassion for them. It was hard to stereotype men after seeing so many different kinds of men to whom I would not ordinarily have been exposed. It was hard to hate someone who had collapsed into tears after an earth-shaking orgasm. Much to my surprise, many men used their time with me to confess secrets and share emotions they were too afraid to tell their family or friends.

After I realized the real reason men were coming to see me, I began educating myself on more than condoms and sexual techniques. I started studying Ancient Sacred Prostitution and sacred sex practices. This gave me a new understanding of my female body and sex. I came to see my vagina as a muscle instead of an orifice. It could be exercised like other muscles, and it could initiate action. I learned that sex could open up mental, emotional, and spiritual doors. I took a class on fire breath orgasms and learned that orgasms could be cultivated simply by the way I breathed. Sex is complex and can be more physical or more spiritual in nature. Who you have sex with isn't as important as how you chose to have sex.

As humans we need to experience wholeness in our lives in order to create a sense of integrity. If we have integrity, we have peace of mind. Cutting ourselves up into little pieces so that our sexual self is separate—from our maternal self, from our spiritual self, and from our work self—causes us to feel scattered at best. It is much more likely to lead to shame, which can attack our core self-esteem. Integrating all these parts of ourselves can create a sense of well-being that has a positive impact on all aspects of our lives, including our sex lives.

I see myself as a sexual, spiritual creature. I envision sex as a creative force, a physical manifestation of the spiritual force of love, and the very core essence of all life. Pleasure is a part of spiritual reality, not a distraction from it. Whether sex takes place at the cellular level when two gametes share chromosomes or genitally when two individuals share orgasms, sex is the blueprint for everything we value and hold dear. It simply is not logical or scientifically sound to see sex as separate from the rest of life. It is the only reason there is life. And if life is sacred simply because it is life, then sex is sacred as well—simply because it is sex.

Since sex simply is sacred by virtue of the fact that it is sex, I don't believe that you have to pursue certain sexual techniques to experience sacred sex. All that is required is a shift in your perception. I found that after I had expunged sexual shame from my life and learned to acknowledge the divine in all people, it was only natural that sex would take on a sacred dimension.

I routinely experienced sacred sex with my clients. Not every man I worked with was open to experiencing the spiritual side of sex. But that did not prevent me from embodying the sacred transformational nature of sex. In fact, it was my insistence upon this shift in perception that catapulted my encounters with men from simply erotic interludes to sex as a healing art. Many of my clients would comment that they felt deep emotions they did not usually associate with the sex act. Whether they were moved to tears or simply perplexed, the fact that they were touched on a spiritual level by the encounter was unmistakable.

If men were only seeking physical release, they would stay home and masturbate for free. Men pay for sex because they desire contact with another human being. Sometimes that desire may become warped or perverted, just as some people marry for selfish and injurious reasons. But many men are seeking something that is missing in their lives. They think maybe it is sex, but they don't know for sure. When they are in the room with an escort, they may be confused as to why they are telling her things they thought they would never tell anyone. They may not have expected to feel so emotional or to shed any tears.

Although each man tends to think he is unique in this respect, sex workers deal with it on a daily basis and know it to be part of the profession. As an escort, I believed I had a sacred trust to treat that vulnerability with respect and to help guide the sexual experience in a direction that was healing, transforming, and uplifting. That is why I was transformed into someone who is inspired by men's sexuality. That is why I no longer see a division between matters of the flesh and matters of the spirit.

Sex took on a spiritual dimension because I opened my heart to it. You can do this, too. But an important prerequisite is the removal of sexual shame. You cannot realize the spiritual potential of sex if you are bound by embarrassment, guilt, or shame. Therapists usually distinguish shame from guilt because shame pertains to your feelings about yourself whereas guilt is about something you have done. Although guilt may serve to guide your moral compass, shame only imbues you with a feeling of being unworthy. When you have unburdened your mind and your life of the useless emotion of shame, then many of the concepts I have approached in this book can come together to create a sacred sexual encounter: healthy boundaries, letting go, meditation, Tantric breathing—even hugging heart chakra to heart chakra.

If all of this seems strange or perhaps overstated, I invite you to read a quote by Deborah Anapol, Ph.D. in Clinical Psychology and the author of *Compersion: Using Jealousy as a Path to Unconditional Love* at www.lovewithoutlimits. com/books.html. Perhaps her words will reach you where mine might have failed: "Sex is sacred because of its role in accessing peak experiences of love, oneness, and healing. Humans have an innate need for peak experiences of bliss, merging, and ecstasy. We have a deep longing for the (re) union of sex and spirit, for union with the Divine. When we access expanded states of consciousness through sex we validate our intuitive sense that sex can be worship and that worship can be erotic. Tantra and other paths of Erotic Spirituality teach us to embrace and honor the body as a temple of Spirit, rather than trying to deny our natural sexual impulses." (from www. lovewithoutlimits.com)

I believe this deep longing for the union of sex and spirit is at least partially responsible for the fact that men continue to see escorts even in this day and age of relatively easy access to free sex. Before the Sexual Revolution, many thought prostitution persisted because of the prevailing morality that encouraged chastity—at least for women. Now there exists another popular explanation, and again it points the finger at women. This time we are to believe that the wives and girlfriends are not good enough or wild enough in bed. This simply is not the truth. Many wives and girlfriends are wonderful in bed, and yet their husbands and boyfriends continue to pay for sex. Many factors contribute to this, and a full explanation exceeds the bounds of this book.

However, several causes are addressed in this book. Certainly the opportunity for at least a momentary freedom from proscribed gender roles—something that many escorts supply on a regular basis to their clientele—ranks very high. This is why I have devoted several chapters to role reversal and techniques for initiating sex. But I have also talked about the desire to pay homage to the female body—female genitals in particular. This desire on the part of men is deeply reverential. What is this reverence if not a form of worship and a desire to experience a merging of the sexual and the spiritual?

Again, if you ask the average client of an escort why he pays for sex, he will invariably tell you that he wants to get off. He might smirk at you for asking such a dumb question, or he might recoil with embarrassment and shame. But whether he is bragging or dodging, none of his responses will accurately reflect his motivations. We simply do not allow for that truth in our culture. And the truth is far too threatening to the myth of male machismo and power. But escorts *do* see the naked truth, and we see it every day.

What I know from 14 years of working with naked men is that they bring far more vulnerability and reverence to the sexual experience with an escort than they would ever want to admit. And after their tears are dried, they can resume the false facade about their masculinity to survive another day in this world as a man. But this window to the truth is not reserved for escorts alone. Almost all wives and girlfriends have witnessed the same dichotomy.

Men do come to women for healing whether they are willing to admit it or not. And it is quite possible and quite natural to achieve healing through sexual union. I believe the sacred transformational nature of sex is apparent not only in the healthy, happy afterglow of post-orgasmic release, but also in the bonding between lovers. Sex can be transformative whenever it enlarges or enriches our life. Sex can be healing whenever it helps us to feel better about anything. And sex can be transformative and healing for both women and men.

I saw this process with my clients time and again. Because most of my professional relationships spanned several years, I was able to see the difference in these men's lives from our first meetings to our last. Mostly what I saw was an opening to life and a blossoming toward healthier self-esteem. Men who had been afraid to ask for a raise might end up getting a promotion or starting their own successful businesses. Men who had felt doomed to live lonely lives devoid of love found the women of their dreams, fell in love, and married.

Did the sex give them courage? Did the love and acceptance I brought to our encounter inspire them to feel better about themselves? Or was the simple act of claiming one's right to pleasure a prelude to other healthy assertion skills? I don't know the answers to those questions. What I do know is that on average, their lives improved. The exception to this was addictive personalities who pursued sex like alcoholics pursue a drink.

Like all addictions, sexual addiction destroys lives. Of course, addiction has no place in a healthy sex life. A definition of addiction is whether a given activity is interfering with your life. So if you are concerned about sexual addiction, you would simply ask yourself if your sexual activities are preventing you from paying your bills, getting to work, having sex with your partner, and so on. Many people fear they have a sexual addiction when they do not. What they are in fact experiencing is sexual shame. Some counselors and spiritual advisors may be quick to label you a sex addict as a reaction to their own sexual shame. Of course, all addicts live in a state of denial, so they are not always the best judges of their own behaviors. But again, look for signs of a dysfunctional life if you suspect addiction. If an individual is functioning well in life, then they are less likely to have a problem with addiction of any kind. And keep in mind that sex gets a bad rap in our current culture, so try not to buy into the shame.

A healthy relationship with our own sexuality can improve our lives in unexpected ways. Sex has a very important connection to our core essences. And healthy sex does seem to improve our self-esteem, serenity, zest for life, and acceptance of others. When you are happy, you feel so much better about the other people in the world. And sex has a way of making us very happy.

What do I mean by "healthy" sex? I mean pretty much the same thing as when I refer to "healthy" food. Healthy food creates life in your body instead of making you sick. Healthy sex creates life in your spirit instead of causing you emotional distress. In the case of sex, you can be fairly assured that it is healthy when it occurs in the context of honest and open communication, mutual consent, clear boundaries, and non-judgmental acceptance (the absence of shame).

It is my hope that you will know freedom from sexual shame, the joy and spiritual fulfillment that make sex sacred, and the union of sex and spirit that fulfill your deepest longings. If improving your sex life ends up transforming your whole life, then so much the better. Whenever and however you explore your sexuality, remember to check in with your intuition and your deepest feelings so you may find your personal sexual path. And may you have a lot of fun along the way!

Afterword

In Search of the Goddess

What is a goddess? The dictionary gives you two choices, either a supernatural being worthy of worship, or a woman of beauty and grace. And, indeed, Western culture has a long history of worshipping women they judge beautiful. For me and many others, the word goddess is much more meaningful than either of these interpretations.

Shortly after becoming an escort, I became interested in and began studying ancient goddess cultures, most of which had a very positive outlook on sex and, coincidentally, women. I read Merlin Stone's landmark book, *When God was a Woman* (Harvest Books, 1978). I flew to England and instead of racing to London like most tourists, I traveled the countryside with my female travel companions looking for ancient sacred Goddess sites such as the stones of Avebury, Chalice Well, and the Tor. I also visited Stonehenge, Silbury Hill, and several castles, but my favorite destination was Glastonbury.

There was something very magical about the week I spent in Glastonbury. My room was a simple bedroom in a bed-and-breakfast, but the window looked out over the heart of the city. Most mornings the mists of Avalon blanketed the buildings, revealing only the beautiful church towers. A little lamb would come to the kitchen each day during our traditional English breakfast of tomatoes, ham, and muffins to suckle from a bottle of milk from the refrigerator.

I toured Glastonbury Abbey, thought by some to be the oldest above-ground Christian church in the world. The Abbey itself is in ruins, but the grounds are beautiful and the Abbot's Kitchen still stands. As I was leaving the Abbot's Kitchen, I spied a large egg-shaped rock rolled against the outside wall of the kitchen. Unlike the Abbot's pot and every other utensil or fixture of the kitchen, this rock had no descriptive name tag or label. Yet it seemed to emanate meaning for me. I felt drawn to the rock, and when I was standing next to it, I wanted to sit upon it. I had no idea why, and it seemed rather inappropriate to do so. What might the groundskeepers or fellow tourists think?

There was a small indentation in the top of the stone. It was the size of a small soup bowl and looked as if it might hold about a cup of whatever. Was this an ancient device for grinding grain? I had no clue. But the impulse to sit on this rock indentation and all would not leave me, so I finally gave in and did just that. Sitting there on that large stone I felt a great peace wash over me as if I were suddenly connected to something ancient and meaningful. But what?

Later that same day, I found a little booklet in a tourist shop with a small paragraph about the stone. Apparently, it predates the Abbey and was used in ancient sacred rituals by the priestesses of old. The rock was meant for menstruating women to sit upon. I was taken aback. How was it that I felt this strong urge to re-enact a rite from so long ago when I was completely ignorant of the ritual or the people who performed it?

Many other magical moments punctuated my stay in Glastonbury. I drank the healing waters of Chalice Well, climbed the Tor under the watch of a full moon, and met many women who were engaged in a similar pilgrimage in search of their connection to the ancient concept of a goddess. I returned home to my life as an escort knowing that it would take years for me to understand and absorb all that I had experienced.

I now know that the menstruation rock held a special significance for me because it was antithetical to the shame I felt for my female body and its normal reproductive and sexual functions. Menstrual blood is taboo. I thought it always had been. I felt a sense of freedom surge through my veins when I learned that long ago women were proud to bleed once a month—they even thought it gave them special creative and intuitive powers. The men of their day actually tried to induce similar powers of perception in themselves through various meditative practices.

How different from today's automatic apology for "being menstrual." Although we may no longer refer to a woman's period as "the curse," the resulting change in a woman's perceptions and emotions is considered negative and undesirable. Oh, we love to hate menstruation. Men complain about it, women endure it, and about the only positive thing you ever hear about it is that it can serve as an indication that you aren't pregnant.

But you can't hate such a major part of being female without having at least a little hostility toward the whole woman. So many of us as women absorb cultural messages that tell us being a woman is not as fun and not as powerful as being male. Studying ancient Goddess cultures opened my mind to a more enlightened view. I learned that females were once considered to be more powerful than males for a variety of reasons, including the fact that new life comes from the womb. When I began to get in touch with my power as a woman, I also started having more fun.

My study of Goddess cultures complemented my study of Ancient Sacred Prostitution. I learned that sex was once thought to be good and potentially healing. The ancient temple priestesses used sex to heal and bless those who came to worship them as the Goddess incarnate. As I absorbed these intriguing aspects of the history of women, being a woman and having sex as a woman took on a whole new dimension for me. Instead of shame, I felt pride. Instead of fear, I felt powerful. Instead of being embarrassed, I was empowered.

As my perceptions about myself shifted, so did my life as an escort. Envisioning myself as the Goddess incarnate, I was able to use sex to heal and bless my clients. In return, my clients blessed me. As my approach to being an escort shifted, so did my clientele. At first, the changes were small.

There was the self-made millionaire who completely refurnished my apartment and put me on an annual retainer. He did not want sex. He liked to talk, order take-out, and watch old movies. My job was to laugh at his jokes and show interest in his stories. It wasn't all that hard to do. He was a kind and generous man who blessed me with many gifts I still enjoy to this day.

Then there was the brilliant doctor with boyish charm who almost fell in love with me. We rendezvoused in New York City where I attended my very first Broadway play. I had a private suite at the Benjamin across from the Waldorf Astoria. The bathroom was solid marble, and the accoutrements were crystal, silver, and china. I always insisted on my own private hotel room when I traveled with clients. I made up for it by not insisting on first-class airfare. But this time he bought first-class airfare for me anyway. I couldn't see wasting all that money just to sit on my butt in the air. So I cashed the tickets in for business class and took the extra $2,000 to a designer boutique.

I wore that sequin gown to the Broadway play. We had a wonderful time in New York. While he was attending business meetings, I worked out in the gym and got massages in the spa. He paid me $18,000 for the 13 hours we actually shared. Of course, I was in New York for two nights and then there was all that time alone on the plane. It was actually a pretty standard fee for high-end escorting. My clients paid for all my travel expenses, too. Hotel, airfare, food, and incidentals were all in addition to my fee. So this date probably ran him about $23,000 total.

Dates like these are not about the sex, although sex is most certainly a part of the date. The actual time in bed was about 3 hours spread over two nights. So if you look at it that way, I was paid more than $10,000 per sexual encounter, or $7,666 per hour of sex. But this kind of number crunching really misses the point about my profession. Escorts and courtesans don't work 40-hour weeks, so you can't get out your calculator and figure out our annual income. One of the perks of working so lucratively is that you don't have to work that frequently.

Before the terrorist attacks of September 11, I had become so spoiled I just expected to catch a plane to a new destination on a regular basis. My trip to a little resort on the Gulf side of Florida found me in a private two-story apartment right on the beach. The azure sea lapped the whitest sand I have ever seen. The scene was so surreal; it seemed more like a postcard than real life. Pelicans flew low while a lone golfer practiced his swing in the distance. Even the seashells and tiny rocks that had washed ashore were pastel pinks, blues, and grays. My benefactor for this date was a film producer who had flown me out for just one night. Our limo took us to a marina restaurant that stayed open past closing just for us. Because we were the only patrons, the chef and staff attended to our every need. I must admit it felt rather decadent having an entire dining establishment to ourselves.

I have quite a few Cinderella stories. Los Angeles, Chicago, Seattle, Princeton, New York, Carmel By-The-Sea, Santa Barbara, and even less glamorous destinations filled my calendar over the span of about two years. It was a different man each time, but all similar dates. Whether we attended the theatre or symphony, toured museums or art galleries, went on shopping sprees for imported lingerie or couture, or simply shared a romantic moonlit walk after dinner, I felt very much like the lead in some fantastic fantasy.

But all the pampering and money in the world would not have made escorting the positive experience it was for me.

Many men offering much more were dismissed before we ever met, due to their bad attitudes. The company I chose to keep had to be uplifting and respectful, or I would have lost my ability to provide a deep and meaningful connection in return. I chose not to base my career on acting skills. I preferred a genuine spiritual connection. And that required that I maintain exquisite boundaries and impeccable standards with and for my clients.

Consequently, I cultivated a group of clients who contributed to my personal growth in ways for which I will never be able to adequately express my gratitude. I became infected with and affected by the many attributes these successful and impressive men possessed. They taught me to see the world through their eyes, and that insight made me a better person. Perhaps the story was not *Cinderella* after all, but *My Fair Lady.*

Although I don't take first-class travel, five-star restaurants, $2,000 dresses, private two-story cottages on the beach, hotel rooms made of marble and mahogany, Broadway plays, limos, shopping sprees, expensive birthday gifts, huge tips, and hot rock massages lightly, money and all that it can buy are not what matters most. The intent and emotions behind these extravagances are more important than the amount of money spent. My feelings about my clients had little to do with the amount of money they spent and everything to do with the energy they brought to our time together. The little things really do make a difference, and heartfelt effort never goes unnoticed.

For instance, I was once greeted with a room filled with incense and meditative music. Goddess figurines abounded, and my eyes were drawn to a simple altar. There, an insignificant amount of money was sandwiched between several CDs. These were not just any CDs. They were the musical creations of my host, and as such, they were deeply personal gifts coming from his core. He creates spiritual music, and his spiritual path is heavy with both Christian and Goddess influences. Consequently, the hour and a half that we shared was like one long prayer, and I was honored to serve as a conduit for the Great Goddess. I left full of joy, peace, and wholeness.

Potent sessions like these transcend the one-dimensional definitions of job or money. And yet the money was an important and integral aspect of the encounter because it served as an offering or symbol of homage. When I think of this client, I feel a warm glow in my heart because he truly knows how to validate women as sexual beings and goddesses. He may not be rich in possessions or wealth, but he is rich in spirit.

During one professional appointment I walked through a client's garden. We marveled over the tomatoes and sweet peas. I bit into a fresh pea pod and quickly devoured the whole thing. Few things are more decadent or delicious than eating vegetables off the vine. He gathered some summer squash and peppers for me to take home with me. Afterward, when I peered into my vegetable crisper, I was fondly reminded of that innocent moment in his garden as well as the tender hugs he bestowed on me while we were together.

It's an old cliché but nevertheless, I have found it to be true: "it's the thought that counts." It really does not matter whether one spends a fortune or nothing at all.

My clients were special to me if they approached me with integrity. Integrity requires that your soul get naked, not just your body. And most of my clients did just that. I could never be exposed to such advanced levels of vulnerability without being forever changed. I have literally been transformed by my clients because of their vulnerability and honesty. My life is richer, and my heart is fuller. Vulnerability, honesty, integrity—they look different on each individual but they are always special.

Another thing that really matters is one's intentions. I have had men double my fee in an attempt to impress me or perhaps feel some sense of power over me. That money is earned the hard way because there is no real connection, just posturing that leaves both people feeling empty. I would much rather a client invest his being and let go enough to truly enjoy himself as well as to take pleasure in my happiness. Sure, the cash comes in handy, but it is small payment for a lousy memory.

Of course, a wealthy man can be just as sincere as a poor man. And some poor men can be just as egotistical and shallow as some rich men. If there is one thing I have learned about men over the last decade and a half, it is that what is in his pocketbook will tell you very little about what is in his heart.

Of course, my ideal client was not defined by his profession, his bank account, or his appearance. He was someone with integrity and sincerity. He was someone who brought an open heart and mind to experiencing either a spiritual dimension to his sexuality or at least an emotional component to his physical gratification. Fortunately, there are so many intriguing and delightful people on this planet that it is really unnecessary to waste time with those who are not.

I simply will not endure the company of a man who is over-bearing, domineering, or shallow. This is especially important when you are spending extended time with an individual. The more time you spend together, the more difficult it becomes to pretend you enjoy someone's company, and if you are not having a good time, neither will your date. This is one of the most important truths about dating, whether for free or a fee. Both people must enjoy themselves, or the date is a bust.

If I am genuinely enjoying myself, there is no need to pretend or fake the enthusiasm and joy I bring to the encounter. I have become so accustomed to experiencing true joy while I am working that I really have no stomach for acting anymore. In the beginning, I did quite a bit of acting and enduring. For a lot lower fee I might add. It is interesting how as one's self-esteem grows and one demands more from life, life will respond by bringing you what you believe you are worth. So my experience of escorting has been that as I raised my rates and insisted upon enjoying my work, I became better at what I did and attracted a much better clientele.

So many of my clients have been honest and generous, not only with their money but with their essences. They have jumped at the opportunity to show their inner selves and peer into me. They have approached life and pleasure as an activity that always has a spiritual dimension. They have learned to abandon themselves to spontaneous moments of joy and mutual bonding. They are able to let go of expectations and control long enough to realize the miracle of each moment. Perhaps experience has taught them that happiness and orgasms are not to be forced but rather welcomed.

I hope that by sharing my journey as an escort and courtesan, I will provide more than just the technical sexual knowledge that I have amassed over the last 14 years. Sex technique is important and takes education and experience to perfect. Certainly, this book has supplied you with some information you can find elsewhere and some tips that only sex workers know. For instance, the Isis Squat is almost never mentioned in sex manuals or sex education classes. This is a truly unique sex technique that I am proud to introduce to you.

But it is most important to me that you absorb the attitudes and emotions that make for a happy sex life. As women, we have unique barriers to our sexual fulfillment, thanks in large part to the sex-negative culture we have grown up in and must live in as adults. I hope that what I have shared with you will assist you in overcoming all obstacles to your total empowerment as a fully sexual woman. As you chart your path to a happy and fulfilling sex life, you may find it helpful to envision yourself as a goddess. It has certainly been central to my transformation.

Claiming our birthright as goddesses is a very powerful and life-changing act. In doing so, we affirm our central role in history as well as our creative influence over the future. On a personal level, we know ourselves to be beautiful inside and outside just as we are. We can reject media messages to the contrary as the money-hungry brainwashing that it is. A goddess is not afraid of getting older because with age comes wisdom and insight. We know that pleasure is not sinful but rather a very special gift—an important aspect of being alive. We feel no shame for our female bodies or our sexual desire. Our roles in life are not to wait, but to take action. Sex is not something that is done to us, it is something we are free to initiate as well as accept. As we reconnect to our inner wisdom and learn to trust our intuition, we can make sexual choices that unite our sexual and spiritual selves, create healing and happiness, and embrace the sensual joy of being alive.

It is my sincere hope that my experiences and insights as an escort will help to enlarge and enrich your sexual world. But most of all, I wish for you true empowerment as the goddess that you are!

Author's Note

The Power of Choice

In the interest of having complete permission for passion and sexual abandon, I have found it necessary to also understand how sex can be harmful. This is required learning for anyone who wants to consider herself an expert in the field of sexual ecstasy!

Saying "yes" to sex and all the joys and pleasures that it can bring is a wonderful, healing, and fulfilling move to make in your life. But I know from personal experience that the joys of sex can be clouded by past experiences that might have been less than happy or consensual. And I also know that you can't really come from a position of power when saying "yes" unless you have first mastered how to say "no." This is especially true for women, who are often encouraged to minimize feelings, needs, and desires, which is simply not a formula that is conducive to creating sexual empowerment.

And as such, any discussion of sexual empowerment is incomplete without addressing sexual abuse and assault. In the course of my escorting career I was sometimes called upon to heal the wounds of sexual abuse in my clients. Of course, that is a long and complex endeavor that requires years of therapy; however, I was able to assist in some small part simply by being sensitive to the issues of sexual abuse and assault survivors. Although a small minority of my clients had been raped or abused either as children or adults, many more of my clients were in relationships with women who had been sexually abused. They came to me because their partners were not available for sex. During our time together, I tried to encourage sensitivity for the difficulties their wives and girlfriends faced on the road to recovery.

Rape and child sexual abuse have a major impact on the lives of both women and men. Whether we are survivors of sexual coercion or we are in a relationship with someone who is, non-consensual sexual activity of any kind has the power to destroy our capacity for joy and peace of mind, as well as our potential for sexual fulfillment. Sexual coercion also takes a toll on society and our attitudes about sex. Because sex can be misused, society and the laws it passes tend to take a dim view of sex in general. This is an unfortunate and unnecessary response to a troubling topic. In fact, if we understand that sexual coercion has more to do with violence and power than it does sex, we can begin to free ourselves to adopt a positive attitude toward sex while despising abuse.

Some disagreement exists regarding statistics for the rate of child sexual abuse. Some claim that one in four girls and one in five boys is sexually abused. A 1997 report by the National Institute of Justice documents that of the 22.3 million children between the ages of 12 and 17 years in the United States, 1.8 million were victims of a serious sexual assault/abuse. No matter to whose statistics you refer, the fact is that an alarming number of children have been traumatized by unwanted and inappropriate sexual contact. These children grow up to be adults who may experience major obstacles to sexual pleasure and intimacy.

Even if you or your partner have never been sexually abused or raped as a child, chances are that at some time in your life—perhaps while you were dating in high school or college—you experienced a less-than-consensual incident. For example, perhaps you said "no," and an ardent suitor forged ahead unabated. Or you might have read a "no" as a "yes" and pursued sexual contact with a less-than-willing partner. Maybe an incident seemed like a misunderstanding or just left a sour taste in your mouth. It is very important to be clear on issues of consent now.

Rape statistics are tallied for persons over the age of 12 and, therefore, data is easier to come by for this group. Of course, not all rapes are reported, and this is particularly true of male rape survivors. The statistics that exist are disturbing enough. One out of every six women in the United States and about 3 percent of men have experienced a rape or a rape attempt (data derived from the Bureau of Justice courtesy of RAINN at www. rainn. org). Rape survivors can encounter a lengthy and difficult recovery process that has a long-term impact on their sexual function.

Rape occurs whenever one person says no to sex and the other person(s) forces them to have sex of any kind. The law will split hairs about the types of sexual contact engaged in, assigning different words and phrases to describe the crime(s) committed, but all you need to know is that unwanted sexual contact of any kind is a crime! You can be raped by someone you know, and you can be raped by someone you have consented to have sex with in the past. You always have the right to say "no" to sex, no matter what you said before. And you have the right to change your mind—during sexual activity. There is no point where it's "too late and you have to go along with sex now because you said you would." You always have the right to say "no." Always.

It is important to note that although childhood sexual abuse and rape at any age can have a profound effect on our sex lives, neither crime is a form of sex. Rapists and child molesters are addicted to an abuse of power. They enjoy the terror, fear, and helplessness of their victims, not the sex act *per se.* In fact, many sexual predators (some estimate 43 percent) do not achieve orgasm during the commission of their crimes.

It is equally important to remember that rape and sexual abuse are never the fault of the victim (or survivor). Anyone can be sexually assaulted, regardless of their gender, race, age, and so on. Because it has nothing to do with the individual who is attacked, there is no logical reason to feel any guilt for being victimized by a perpetrator. Knowing this can facilitate the healing process for many survivors.

Prior to my career as an escort, I was not able to enjoy sex as much as I can today. Even my sex life with my boyfriend was tenuous at best because of some issues I had yet to sort out. If he came up from behind me while I was washing the dishes, I would freak out, becoming angry and fearful. If his leg brushed against mine while we were sleeping in the same bed, my skin would crawl. I knew I trusted him. I knew I was attracted to him. So what was the problem?

I took the issue to my therapist, and she helped me to understand that these were the natural reactions of someone who had survived sexual trauma. You see, I am a survivor of both incest (sexual abuse/molestation by a family member/authority figure) and rape. Although my adolescence was a promiscuous one, I rarely enjoyed the act of sex. Rather, I pursued affection and validation via sexual contact. The sex act itself was an experience I endured in order to feel loved, but I couldn't enjoy sex because my mind was numb.

Several things helped me to go from being nonorgasmic and numb to having multiple orgasms and being full of sexual joy. The most important factor was therapy. I cannot stress enough how crucial long-term therapy is for any survivor of sexual trauma. My therapist helped me to go through the stages of grieving that are such an integral part of the healing process.

A violation of our sexual selves attacks us at our core, and it makes it extremely difficult to trust or let go, which are necessary ingredients for a happy sex life. Therapy gave me a sense of myself as the final arbiter of my body. I learned about healthy boundaries—something incest survivors are trained away from by their perpetrators. I learned to trust myself instead of others. If my intuition told me to get away from someone or some situation, I heeded the warning instead of telling myself "but he seems like such a nice guy," or "I'm sure he means well." My feelings and my safety became more important than being polite or nice.

I had to go through a period of sexual abstinence to get well. Refraining from sex allowed me to connect with my center and feel whole alone. As a survivor of childhood sexual abuse, I needed to experience myself in an asexual way before I could connect with my sexuality. I had been cheated out of an innocent childhood, so I decided to reclaim it. I became a good parent to myself and gave myself the love and validation that I had deserved as a young girl. Some things, like buying myself a Barbie doll and a Tonka truck, might seem silly, but they went a long way to heal my inner child. Because of the healing that I experienced while being abstinent, I embrace abstinence as not only a valid sexual choice, but an important stop on the road to sexual wholeness. You must learn to say "no" before you can truly say "yes."

I also took a wonderful self-defense class that was tailor-made for women, called Model Mugging. There were about 16 women in the class, and we learned to defend ourselves from a would-be assailant who was dressed in a padded suit. The man in the "mugger's suit" endured our full-impact kicks and punches while we learned to back up our "NO" with more than words. It was a wonderful experience for many reasons. The class taught healthy boundaries and how not to "give up space" to an attacker. We got to yell and scream and cry, if need be. Many of us had been in scary situations in real life, and it was great to get to talk about it, feel the love and support of the staff and our classmates, and re-enact situations in which we had felt powerless in the past. This time we prevailed.

My sense of self and my self-worth improved drastically because of all these factors: therapy, abstinence, and self-defense. You might think these a strange collection of cures for sexual dysfunction, but each was a vital component in the foundation of my recovery. After I had attained a level of comfort and confidence, I was ready for "hands-on" healing. I was now empowered to say "yes" to sex on my terms.

By the time I became an escort and a married woman, I had made a great deal of progress in reclaiming my sexual response. I had been in intensive therapy specifically for incest and rape survivors for about 5 years. I still had more work to do. I wasn't numb anymore, but I knew I could experience even more sexual pleasure if I could just get past the sexual trauma. I was intent on doing just that. Because I felt that if I didn't my perpetrators would have succeeded in victimizing me twice—once when they sexually abused me and a second time by intruding on my sex life by making it dysfunctional—I was not about to let those evil individuals take my sex life away from me.

I continued with therapy. I also found that my work as an escort was a wonderful healing tool for me. I am not recommending it for others—just sharing that it was an important part of my personal journey to sexual wholeness. I found it particularly healing to be able to apply the "head knowledge" that therapy imparted to me in a "hands-on" way.

Practicing my boundaries, saying "yes" and saying "no," changing my mind in the middle of a sexual encounter, and learning to trust myself instead of my partner were all integral steps toward reclaiming my body. Certainly, these are things one can practice in a long-term committed relationship as well. And I recommend that *all* women do just that, whether they have experienced nonconsensual sex or not. It is a lesson in self-reliance and assertion skills from which most all women can benefit.

I was able to share this personal journey with my clients as well. If they were in a relationship with a woman who was having difficulty enjoying sex because of a traumatic sexual experience in her past, they gained some insight and empathy into her situation by listening to mine. Perhaps if they were inclined to be kind in the first place, they would now be able to show a little more patience and love. If, however, it was my male client who was suffering from a past sexual trauma, he often realized he would require therapy before he could hope to completely reclaim his sexual function and joy. And I also created a safe and accepting environment for him while we were together.

How does one create a safe environment for a survivor of sexual coercion? First and foremost, it is vital to listen. People who have been abused may have difficulty expressing their feelings. They may speak quietly or invalidate themselves at every turn. They may simply fail to speak up at all and go into "shut-down" mode at the first sign of conflict. If you want to be helpful, you must remain quiet and give them a chance to speak. If they still say nothing, then assure them it is safe to say whatever they want, and that you will not judge or argue with their feelings. Be prepared for a certain amount of anger. Anger is a natural part of the healing process. In this manner, you can create emotional safety.

The second most important thing you can offer a survivor of nonconsensual sex is physical safety. Never touch any part of their body without prior permission. That includes their hair, shoulders, arms, hands—anything! It can be very difficult for survivors to feel that they own their bodies. You can help by acknowledging that they own every bit of their bodies and have complete and total control of them. Just because it was okay for you to touch them in a certain way yesterday does not mean it is okay to touch them that way today. Just ask. May I hug you? May I hold your hand? And never assume their answer will be "yes." Listen for their answer and accept it with a sincere smile no matter what their response. Survivors need to feel loved and accepted, no matter if they say "yes" or "no."

Working with male survivors, I was very careful to ask permission to touch them—even though they were paying me for sex. I never assumed any type of touch was okay unless I had specific permission to touch them there and in that way. Usually, after we had progressed to the point of actually having sex (oral or intercourse), we had stopped talking and were into the action. But if I wanted to do something like touch his rectum or get on top of him, I would again ask for permission. I might even avoid certain sexual acts, such as the Isis Squat,

270

because they are so overpowering. But I never assumed that they could handle something just because they were men. Those types of assumptions had no place in my work as an escort.

Again, whether you are a survivor, your partner is a survivor, or neither of you is a survivor—being familiar with this topic is very important to your personal life. If you are informed about nonconsensual sex, you can separate that issue from issues about sexual freedom and autonomy. This will impact how you relate to yourself and your partner, how you raise your children, and even how you vote. Anyone who would like to consider themselves well-informed or experienced in the sexual arena must be versed in the topic of sexual coercion as well. Having a complete understanding of what is required for consensual sex can open the doors to guilt-free passion and fearless sexual bliss!

And finally, it is important that women realize that nothing they could ever do or say or be would ever justify an act of sexual coercion. That includes being sexually promiscuous and/or dressing in a "provocative" manner. What can you do about fears of being "too slutty?"

Most women have grown up investing a great deal of energy attempting to control and hide their sexual wholeness. We live in constant fear of what others will think (and perhaps do) if they perceive our clothing is "too revealing" or find out that we enjoy sex "too much." Each woman has a different defini-tion of what it means to be "a slut." But nonetheless, a hier-archy exists between the "good girls" and the "bad girls." This sexual double standard, which is only applied to women—not men—is damaging for many reasons. For the purposes of this book, the most pertinent reason is that it has a deleterious effect on the enjoyment of all sex—even monogamous married sex in the missionary position.

If women are afraid of appearing to be sluts before motherhood, I think that fear is quadrupled after having children. It is as if some women forget how they got pregnant in the first place. Society puts a great deal of pressure on mothers to at least appear sexually "pure."

The important thing to remember is that you are a sexual being with every right to respect and dignity as a sexual being. Derogatory terms such as "slut" are intended to shame and control you, but you don't have to buy into them. The word "slut" creates a lot of hurt and harm for women, so I choose NOT to give it any power. I believe that nothing a woman does can make her a slut. But if people want to use that word, then I will wear it with pride. In the interest of reclaiming my right to sexual fulfillment and joy, I created a totally new and empowering definition for the word "sluts:"

<u>S</u>exual

<u>L</u>iberated

<u>U</u>nique

<u>T</u>alented

<u>S</u>isters!

Resources

Like I said in the introduction to this book, sex is a big topic about which you can always learn more. The following resources are some of my favorite places to find sexual information, sex toys, and sexual fun. Enjoy!

Free Online Information about Sex, Sexual Health, and Relationships

Femmerotic Network
(just for women!)
www.scarletletters.com/current/femmerotic.html

The Institute for 21st Century Relationships
(articles about alternative coupling)
www.lovethatworks.org/index.html

International Academy of Sex Research
(informative journal)
www.iasr.org

Jane's Guide
(book, video, and website reviews; articles and much more!)
www.janesguide.com

The Kama Sutra Temple
(very detailed information about Kama Sutra and Tantra!)
www.tantra.org

The Kinsey Institute
(tons of info!)
www.indiana.edu/~kinsey

Libido: The Journal of Sex and Sensibility
(erotic writing and art at its finest)
www.libidomag.com

National Sexuality Resource Center
(intelligent and current articles)
http://nsrc.sfsu.edu/Index.cfm

Safer Sex
(and more!)
www.safersex.org

San Francisco Sex Information
(phone or e-mail with your questions—for FREE!!)
www.sfsi.org

Sex Education for the Real World
(targeting teens)
www.scarleteen.com

Sexuality Information and Education Council
of the United States
(sexual rights)
www.siecus.org/index.html

Society for Human Sexuality
(everything you ever wanted to know)
www.sexuality.org

Spiritual Sexuality
(workshops and articles)
www.spiritualsexuality.com

How to Cure Vaginal Infections
(homemade remedies that really work!)
www.ehow.com/how_7838_cure-vaginal-infections.html

Expert Assistance, Classes, and Informative Videos

American Association of Sex Educators, Counselors, and Therapists
(find a sex therapist in your area)
www.aasect.org

Better Sex Videos by Sinclair Institute
(instructional and erotic couples' videos)
www.bettersex.com/default.asp

The Body Electric
(training in touch)
www.bodyelectric.org

The Institute for Advanced Study of Human Sexuality
(get a degree in sex!)
www.iashs.edu

The New School of Erotic Touch
(instructional books, videos, and DVDs)
www.eroticmassage.com/cgi-bin/shop.cgi

Sexological Bodyworkers
(schedule an appointment or enroll in a class)
www.sexologicalbodywork.com

Online Shopping

Toys in Babeland
(woman-friendly!)
www.babeland.com

Good Vibrations
(the original woman-friendly store!)
www.goodvibes.com

Woman-Produced Porn
(romantic and explicit!)
www.royalle.com

Libida—Toys, Tips, and Erotica for Women
(ask a sexpert and treat yourself to a new toy)
www.libida.com

Beauty Tips, Erotic Art, Lingerie, and so on
(read the video reviews or join the debate about younger men)
http://sex-kitten.net

Woman-Friendly Adult Stores

Adam & Eve
6311 Glenwood Avenue
Raleigh, NC 27612
919-571-7209
Visit AdamEve.com/stores for listings of additional locations
in: Winston-Salem, Charlotte, Greensboro, and Durham.

Eve's Garden
119 West 57th Street
New York, NY 10019
1-800-848-3837

Toys in Babeland
707 E. Pike Street
Seattle, WA 98122
206-328-2914

Toys in Babeland
94 Rivington Street
New York, NY 10003
212-375-1701

Toys in Babeland
43 Mercer Street
New York, NY 10012
212-966-2120

Good Vibrations
603 Valencia Street
San Francisco, CA 94110
1-800-BUY-VIBE

Grand Opening!
318 Harvard Street, Suite 32
Brookline, MA 02446
617-731-2626

Grand Opening!
8442 Santa Monica Boulevard
West Hollywood, CA
323-848-6970

A Woman's Touch
600 Williamson Street
Madison, WI 53703
608-250-1928

Ruby's Pearl
323 E. Market Street
Iowa City, IA 52245
319-248-0032

Early To Bed
5232 N. Sheridan Road
Chicago, IL 60640
773-271-1219

Communities and Clubs

The Center for Sex and Culture
(social gatherings and workshops in San Francisco)
www.centerforsexandculture.com

Club Cake for Women
(sexual culture as entertainment for women)
www.cakenyc.com

The Museum of Sex
(the only one of its kind in America—a must-see if you
are in NYC)
www.museumofsex.com

The Wet Spot
(social gatherings and workshops in Seattle)
www.wetspot.org

The Woodhull Freedom Foundation
(sexual rights for women and everyone!)
www.woodhullfoundation.org